Publishing as a Marketing Strategy

Authoring a book to attract
ideal clients through credibility
as an expert

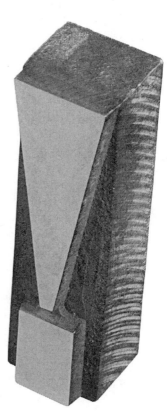

by Joan Boneberg, Bonnie Daneker, Robin Hensley,
Vanessa Lowry, Ahmad Meradji and Anita Paul

First Edition Printed, 2011

Published by: **BookLogix Publishing Services, Inc.**
www.booklogix.com

Cover Art and Layout Design by: **Vanessa Lowry**
www.connect4leverage.com

Cover Photo: © **Marek Uliasz | Dreamstime.com**

This book may be purchased in bulk for educational, business, fundraising
or sales promotional use. For information please contact:
Vanessa Lowry, www.connect4leverage.com

This book is designed to provide accurate information in regard to the subject
matter covered. It is sold with the understanding that the publisher is not
engaged in rendering legal, accounting or other professional services. If
you require legal advice or other expert assistance, you should seek the
services of a competent professional.

Library of Congress Control Number: 2011919590

ISBN: 978-1-61005-114-9

Printed in the United States of America

Acknowledgements

This book is a result of the contribution of many entreprenuers and consultants who have used authoring as a successful tool for marketing.

Thanks to my friend Robin Kirby for suggesting I create a collaborative book on this topic. I'm grateful for our weekly idea exchange, laugh fest and encouragement over early morning coffee.

Thank you to my fellow co-authors: Joan Boneberg, Bonnie Daneker, Robin Hensley, Ahmad Meradji and Anita Paul. You made this book journey easy and interesting. Thanks to my LinkedIn community, to the second and third level of connection, who answered my question regarding publishing as a marketing strategy ... and for allowing me to include your responses in this book.

To my husband, Ben Lowry for editing the first draft of this book and his support throughout the project. To Lisa Wright and Bonnie Daneker for subsequent edits and review as the book came to life.

It takes a village to publish a book. I appreciate all the lovely people who choose to be part of the Vanessa Village, who help me get my ideas out of my head and who make the effort worthwhile.

~Vanessa Lowry

Table of Contents

Chapter 1
Establishing Expert Status

expert (noun)

> a person who has a comprehensive and authoritative knowledge of or skill in a particular area: *experts in child development | a financial expert.*

Tools used for marketing have evolved at a rapid pace over the past several decades. As technology has developed, the ways to creatively use that technology for marketing has expanded.

In the mid 1980s, the introduction of the fax machine led to companies sending advertising messages by fax. Infomercials were developed as cable television channels began to launch. Advertisers could now more affordably purchase on-air time targeted to a particular market segment. These commercials in the guise of an informational program are still an effective way for many companies to promote a particular product or service to a niche market.

A subset of telemarketing is text message advertising sent to cell phones, and with satellite communication, businesses can contact potential buyers worldwide. The internet has created hundreds of ways to also promote to prospects beyond your local reach. Some of these online methods include email marketing, interactive websites, pay-per-click ad words, banner ads, and a myriad of forms of social media.

Every business needs a way to reach new customers. Business professionals and consultants who are perceived as experts find it easier to attract ideal clients while having the flexibility to charge a premium for their services.

A published book remains a powerful way to establish status as an expert. Authors of business books have always enjoyed an expanded perception of credibility. A book represents a specific viewpoint or information as a snapshot in time. Some books are published with content that is timeless for decades while others represent constantly changing information.

Until just a few years ago, writing and publishing a book was out of reach for many business professionals. Digital printing has made it easier and more affordable to share your unique perspective and business knowledge with prospects and clients. Many business professionals, including the authors of this book, find that having a published book serves as a powerful introduction to prospects in new segments of business or new industries at a higher level.

In gathering author experiences for this book, this question was posted on LinkedIn: *"In what ways has publishing a book helped you market your business?"* Some of the comments included:

- Helped me organize and crystallize my thinking in specific areas of expertise

- Invites interest to my point of view

- Draws attention of media and prospective clients

- Boosts business revenues

- Serves as a keepsake and refresher for those who attend training I facilitate

- Is a distinguishing feature in a competitive proposal

2

- Provides a shorthand introduction to my capabilities
- Serves as an expanded business card
- Lends credibility to my programs
- Increased my professional credibility
- Contributed to my reputation as a thought leader
- Promotes my brand
- Established my expertise internationally
- Allows my message and proficiency to be communicated to a broader audience
- Leaves a legacy of thought and insight
- Helps position me as an expert in my field
- Demonstrates my knowledge, level of commitment in my field and my ambition
- Sets me apart when compared to my competition
- Creates opportunities for more word-of-mouth marketing
- Produces requests to comment on my topic(s) for articles
- Generates invitations to speak to businesses, groups and conferences
- Provides diverse opportunities for marketing over multiple years
- Requests for interviews on television and radio
- People take more interest and ask more informed questions

See complete answers from LinkedIn respondents of this question in Appendix II titled "Other Contributors."

The marketing consultancy Rain Group, headed by Mike Schultz and John Doerr, surveyed 200 business book authors who have written over 590 books. The resulting report, *The Business Impact of Writing a Book*, yielded these statistics:

- 56% of authors reported a "Strong" or "Very Strong" influence on their ability to generate more leads for their services.
- 63% of authors reported a "Very Strong" or "Strong" influence on generating new clients.

In an interview with Karen Klein of *Business Week*, Mr. Schultz stated that "The vast majority of the authors we surveyed — 96% — said they did realize a significant positive impact on their businesses from writing a book and would recommend the practice."[1] Find out more about their published report at *www.RainToday.com*.

Publishing a book can be leveraged into paid speaking engagements. The National Speakers Association reports that 55% of its 3,000 members are authors and more than half earn $5,000+ for a full day engagement.[2]

The Wall Street Journal published an article exploring the topic of entrepreneurs and professionals embracing self publishing to burnish credentials, attract new clients and even create celebrity for the author. According to the article, psychiatrist Dr. Ish Major has been a guest on the "Today" show twice since self publishing his book, *Little White Whys: A Woman's Guide Through the Lies Men Tell and Why*.[3]

As you read *Publishing as a Marketing Strategy*, you will find many perspectives and experiences on the business impact of writing a book. You may decide publishing is a business decision worth exploring. Please connect with the authors of this book if their particular expertise will be helpful to you.

The first section includes chapters that are arranged alphabetically by author with the exception of the chapter by Ahmad Meradji. His chapter walks the reader through the process of publishing and begins on page 63.

The appendix sections include books, blogs, tips and comments from other business professionals who have published books along with bios of the authors of this book.

It's been said that writing a book is like presenting a very large business card to your audience: it introduces you, explains your area of expertise, and provides a channel for follow-up questions. You have the knowledge and the drive. With this book, you will have the information you need to add that very large business card to your marketing arsenal to position yourself to be known as the expert you are.

---

[1] *Karen E. Klein, "Business by the Book," Business Week, April 12, 2006*

[2] *Andrea DiMickele, "Spotlight: Business Of Speaking Revealed," PRWeb, March 29, 2011*

[3] *Sarah E. Needleman, "As You May Have Read in My Book," The Wall Street Journal, December 31, 2010*

Chapter 2
Take The Opportunity

Joan M. Boneberg, *M.S., CCC-SLP, Executive Communication Coach, ASHA Board Certified Speech Pathologist, Certified Accent Reduction Specialist and author, is CEO of Speech Improvement Resources, LLC. She specializes in assisting executives who have a career need or personal desire to become effective and skillful communicators. Joan can be reached at **www.speakingspecialist.com** or 678.522.5955.*

In 1984, the year I finished graduate school, I decided someday I would have my own business communication firm and write a book. I didn't know when that day would arrive, but I had faith that it would. I did not focus on a particular year to accomplish these goals because I wanted the timing to be right. It was important to me to feel it was the right time and have it be a natural extension of the next phase in my career. My highest priority was to increase awareness of the power of communication and the positive impact it can have on people's professional and personal lives. It was also very important to me to enjoy and appreciate the process. After twenty four years, it felt right. For me things aligned internally and externally. It was a feeling of "rightness." That's all I needed, so in April 2008, I launched my communication firm, Speech Improvement Resources, LLC. In October 2009, I began my book, *Communication Chemistry: 25 Essential Elements to Make You a Compelling Communicator.* It really was a "pinch me" moment.

My decision to move forward with my book project was based on various strategic reasons: to increase my visibility in the marketplace, gain corporate training opportunities, and use the book as the center of my coaching. I felt confident about writing the book because I knew my communication message and the way I formatted the book were not typical. I began at that time because it felt right to write it.

When I approach a project that is complex with many "moving parts" such as writing a book, I brainstorm a logical sequence of tasks that will result in the desired outcome. Of course, within that framework is the need to have the willingness to monitor and adjust along the way. I have found being open to various ideas during this phase increases the chances of creativity within the process.

When considering writing a book as a marketing tool for your business, it's essential to make sure you have your heart fully in it. If you decide to move forward, compose a marketing strategy you can fully embrace before you commit your heart, time, effort, energy and financial resources to the project. If these issues are not addressed thoroughly before writing, the process and the end result most likely will not be what you wanted them to be or what they could have been.

When marketing a book one needs to think strategically. Questions such as, "What is the target audience?", "Where do I want to market: locally, regionally, nationally, internationally?", "Do I want to try to have my book available in stores or just on the internet?" etc. Of course, many other questions need to be asked and answered with honesty so these issues will not become problematic. In my opinion, marketing is the most challenging part of publishing a book. One needs as much creativity in marketing the book as in the writing of it.

My philosophy of "why not?" was at the heart of my marketing efforts. When I sat down to list marketing strategies and goals, I let my brain take over to list as many different ideas as I could think of even if I initially thought it was "out of my league" or it "would never happen."

My first thought was, "How can I market my book with the 'vehicles" I already have? My initial desire was to diversify my marketing efforts without incurring any additional cost. My first strategy was to use my existing website, *www.speakingspecialist.com* and include a separate "book" page. My intention was to give the visitors to my website the opportunity to see examples of the content and format of my book. In addition to creating a "book" page, I also created a "media page" in order to demonstrate the interest in my book.

A related advantage I received from this approach resulted in an increase in my page ranking for my business on Google, Bing, AOL, etc. It has been noticeably helpful because there has been an increase in individuals contacting me to seek my communication coaching services as well as requests for presentations with opportunities for "back of the room sales." It has definitely increased my revenue stream.

The opportunity to market my book using my existing platforms (i.e. my professional and personal networks, memberships in organizations, networking events, social media, etc.) has given me various venues to discuss my book without the tremendous cost of "overhead." With access to an array of internet tools, book marketing has not only become significantly less costly and more efficient, but its ability to reach a broader spectrum of potential readers is amazing.

Of course, the use of social media is a wonderful way to market without any cost involved. I set up Facebook, Twitter and You Tube accounts solely for marketing my business and book. Social media is another great way to increase your visibility as well as a wonderful way to integrate your website, videos, newsletters and upcoming events you want to cross promote to increase your exposure.

Networking has been a very large part of my marketing efforts. Since I'm a "people person," it was natural that I focused on it. There is a huge advantage in networking for marketing purposes. The opportunity to meet so many people from different professions, interests and needs is an outstanding way to increase contacts. Generally, people have a fascination when meeting someone who has written a book. It often seems to be a natural conversation starter. Networking provides a perfect way to increase interest and build relationships.

My strong desire to have a nationally-known bookseller accept my book was a dream of mine. One afternoon, as I was driving past this very well known and highly visible bookseller, I decided to turn around, park and take my book in the store. I reminded myself of my mantra, "Why not?" I asked the manager, "How can I get the right set of eyes to look at my book?" He gave me the phone number of their small press division in their New York City Headquarters. When I arrived home, I called the headquarters and wrote down their requirements for submission. As I composed the required cover letter, again my mantra popped into my head, "Why not?"; "Why not me?"; "It **is** possible they would accept my book."

On November 1, 2010, I packaged my book with the cover letter included and mailed it at the post office. As I placed the package in the out-going mail slot, I thought, "If I receive a response in three to four months indicating my book was received, that would be great!" Seven weeks after I submitted my book, I received my acceptance letter! Having the most well known retail bookseller in the United

States accept my first book was one of the biggest thrills I've ever had! I felt extreme joy, pride and confirmation my book was well done with an important and strong message. It definitely was a "pinch me" moment.

It has been very gratifying to see my book doing exactly what I intended it to do; capture the attention of corporate level professionals, attract more clients for communication services and have opportunities to increase my visibility in media (i.e. guest interviews and guest hosting on internet radio, participating in videos and newspaper interviews and a tele-seminar).

One lesson I have learned about book marketing is this: begin to market the book very early on in the process. Do not wait until you have the final copy in your hand. If you market early and keep your potential readers posted on a consistent basis you will begin to attract a loyal following. That is the key to building a platform of potential clients.

I'm very excited to begin planning my next book. Now that I have the experience of writing, publishing and marketing a book, I will approach my follow-up book knowing the right questions to ask and the ability to tweak my marketing plan.

My strong belief is, without thorough preparation, the chances of success are significantly diminished.

My marketing plan will continue to include the strategies I used for my first book. However, I will increase the use of social and traditional media as well as opportunities for book signings and speaking engagements for professionals, which are my target audiences.

There is no denying it, writing a book as a part of your business marketing will increase your visibility, opportunities and revenue if done right. Additionally, using the approach and attitude of "Why not?" helps with marketing efforts immensely. If you realize very early in the process the need to be creative in your marketing approach, it will increase your book's visibility and provide additional opportunities.

You may feel some of the larger opportunities to market are not within your reach, but if you are prepared and take the attitude of "Why not?" surprising things may happen. Your attitude and approach can make or break your success. The thought of writing a book for your business should not be a drudgery. If you are considering writing a book, it needs to be written for the right reasons.

If you approach the process in that way, it will serve you well and will continue to pay you dividends.

My thought regarding writing a book is this: it's about being so passionate you cannot help but write down your message and share it with others.

*Take on the attitude of
"Why not" and become so
passionate about your topic that
you must share it with others.*

~Joan Boneberg

Chapter 3
More Than a Marketing Tactic:
Writing a Book Can Change Your Career and Your Life

As CEO of Write Advisors, **Bonnie B. Daneker** *oversees the strategic direction of the company to enable its clients to express themselves digitally and in print, using the most appropriate resources to reach their non-fiction publishing goals.* **www.writeadvisors.com**

Dear Aspiring Author,

I've heard through the grapevine that you've been thinking about writing a book. Good for you. Let's talk.

There are many personal reasons for writing a book. It's been on your "Bucket List." You're raising money for a cause. You're hoping to connect with others of like interests. Or maybe you'd just like to create conversation at cocktail parties.

There are many professional reasons, too. Maybe you'd like to raise your visibility. Position yourself as an expert. You know this will increase credibility with clients and secure new prospects. Or maybe you'd like to join the speaking circuit. Meet peer authors and established authorities. Or the biggest reason of them all, you'd like a new career focus — a new role or new business.

Whatever your motivation, it's important for you to know a little secret: despite all the advances in technology, books remain one of the most powerful communications vehicles ever created. If you're thinking about writing a book, *don't take it lightly.* It can, and will, change your life and your work. And, if done well, your book can impact the lives and work of others, too.

How do I know, you might wonder?

Well, I know because it's happened to me. Not once, not twice, but seven times. Each time I learn a little more. I'm still writing, and thank heavens, I'm not done learning.

I'm with you today to share a little of my story. I'm hoping you don't repeat the mistakes I made and you can adopt some of the good practices as your own.

So let me take you back a few years, to 1999, when we were all uncertain about the disruptions the millennial change would bring. As a technology consultant, I teamed with other skilled Year 2000 (or Y2K) professionals to safeguard computer operations at CheckFree, the largest financial transaction processing company in the nation. Our goal was to ensure that after January 1, 2000 everyone could still access their money: ATM cards would work. We could still buy groceries with debit cards. Still pay at the pump with credit cards. Thankfully, with careful planning and intense follow through, we transitioned with few glitches.

Months later, my father was diagnosed with cancer. Though I'd always had an interest in medicine, helping him became my priority. I was grateful able to continue my consulting responsibilities remotely, which allowed me to concentrate on his care. Resources to help me were limited: the internet was so young and books to help caregivers of cancer patients were so few. I found comradeship in other caregivers as we waited in hospital lobbies and doctors' offices. You would be surprised at the nuggets of knowledge that come your way if you pay attention.

With their wisdom and support from professionals who would become part of my Medical Advisory Board, I wrote and published my first book, *The Compassionate Caregiver's Guide to Caring for Someone with Cancer.* This is not my story, but a collection of advice for any caregiver helping a patient through cancer diagnosis, treatment, and post-treatment changes. Essentially, I wrote the book that I needed – but more importantly, that so many others needed. The statistic from American Cancer Society is that for every one person diagnosed with cancer, an average of five others are affected (spouse, children, friends, co-workers, etc.). And, more than 800,000 people get diagnosed each year – you can do the math. I hope you never need it, but if you do it's there, and you can find it on **www.amazon.com**.

My career direction took a radical turn as I left the world of technology. Because of the tremendous demand for caregiver knowledge, I was distributing copies everywhere. I was speaking at cancer-related functions. I finished the Susan G. Koman Walk for the Cure. I was on the Executive Committee for St. Joseph's Cancer Survivors' Network. I was suddenly immersed in a world of pain and misery to which I could positively contribute. I wanted to help, and through my book I could. Later, I founded my own publishing company to reach caregivers faster, at their access points – a web site, support group materials, in-hospital care packets, Care Team folders for the primary caregivers. I hadn't planned to offer these other products and services, but they were natural extensions of our content. Things like this can and do happen.

Continuing to write, I covered heady subjects: *Understanding the Cancer Diagnosis, Handbook on Hospice and Palliative Care, A Cancer Patient's End of Life, The Journey of Grief,* and *The Journeys of Grief After Trauma.* With each publication, I learned more about the disease and had a certain comfort level in discussing it.

However, I learned something even more valuable: how to communicate with others in a language they could process. Stricken by the cancer diagnosis in a loved one, my readers would often suffer from unclear thinking, distraction and worry. My writing skills were forced to improve, as my readers would ask me questions or demand more detail. If you listen to your readers, your writing will improve as well.

I learned another lesson very quickly: although you may be a competent individual contributor, you cannot do it all yourself. I hired Julie Simon, the best editor I know, to review my manuscripts. Highly competent, she polished them until they shone. It wasn't cheap and it wasn't easy, but it was an investment well worth it. I hired several other wonderful resources to add to the book design and presentation. I also hired a publicist, who worked with me to create a top-notch marketing plan but I soon discovered planning and execution were two separate things, and not all people are good at both. I've already mentioned my Medical Advisory Board... I'd recommend you populate a bench of professionals to help you with your book.

There were personal changes with my first book, too. I have to take a moment to acknowledge my fantastically-supportive husband and surgical oncologist extraordinaire. I certainly wasn't looking for a date when I met him at a benefit for American Cancer Society. But I was looking for a source to help me complete the parts on how to prepare for "resection" or removal of cancer tumors through surgery. He not only helped me with those sections, but he reviewed *nearly all* my text and introduced me to many of his colleagues. I tell you this because, as you're dreading doing the background work necessary to support your book with sound facts as evidence, you'll know that research can be fun if you pick the right partner (and can be even better when you fall in love!).

So, continuing the story: my status changed to wife, stepmom, and puppy mom, in addition to President of a publishing house, all because of my first book.

By the time my sixth book rolled around, I understood the nuances on how to structure content. Our mission – "Providing tools and support for your caregiving journey" (our company's tagline) – had been accomplished, and I was ready for a new challenge. *Journeys of Grief After Trauma* was written in partnership. The professionals at the university medical center that sponsored the work saw similarity between grieving for cancer patients and grieving in other trauma situations. The context was this: having a potentially terminal disease or caring for a loved one with that disease is equally traumatic to experiencing a severe auto accident, being disfigured, or losing one of your senses. Something that continues to surface in this research is that we grieve for the immediate loss, what we knew to be true that isn't true now, and the loss of what could have been. Writing this was exhausting, not cathartic and energizing, as many of the other pieces were. The message to me was crystal clear: It was time to move on. In writing your book, you may discover yourself changing and you should be aware of the opportunities that present themselves as a result of your work.

I do take my own advice...when Sandy Hoffman asked me to help out on the flagship publication for Women in Technology (WIT), I jumped at the task. A mentor and friend in addition to being the President of the organization, Sandy is one person people can't say "No" to. The seventh book was up and running. As a marketing tool, *CLIMB: Leading Women in Technology Share Their Journeys to Success* is the most effective piece I've had the privilege to contribute to.

Over 60 people are profiled in the book, each with a personal style. An added bonus to this type of anthology, each "contributor" brought a personal promotions suitcase: extensive personal and professional networks, impressive education, vast corporate or entrepreneurial experience, and oftentimes prior publicity. Our book sale blast – over 1,000 sold in the first six weeks after launch – was largely due to these assets. (It's now in its second printing.) The book was written to give exposure to our members and supporters in the Atlanta technology community. Additionally, it is a fundraiser for our Girls Get IT programs. These programs foster interest in STEM careers (Science, Technology, Engineering and Math) from girls 12-18. Through our book sales and other donations, we were able to give a $10,000 check to support local FIRST Robotics programs. If you're interested in purchasing a copy, you can order it at **www.mywit.org**.

We have found ourselves in a wonderful snowball of publicity. Our efforts to promote *CLIMB* and benefit other girls' organizations led to media coverage and activities we hadn't put in our original marketing plan. Here's a sampling of the marketing opportunities that surfaced within six months after publication of our book:

- Moderating Panels/ Panel Discussion
- Corporate Speaking Events
- Local Radio, Online Radio
- Webinars and Podcasts
- Book Club Readership
- Newsletters and Blogs
- Local Media
- Girls' and Women's Groups
- Local and National University Publicity
- Technology Trade Media Coverage

- Mentorship Organizations
- Social Media Promotions
- Direct Publicity from Employers of Contributors
- Science, Technology, Engineering, and Math Career Associations Interest
- Local Bookstores Book Signings
- WIT Forums and Website Exposure

A lesson here is to determine your balance between proactive and reactive measures in promotions (Proactive meaning those you plan for, reactive meaning those you don't). Someone once told me "Word of Mouth follows Word of Mouse," which means that if you do some careful planning and execution upfront, other opportunities will surface. You need to consider all those other opportunities but find the balance between them and what you've already planned to do. It's easier to keep track of your marketing dollars and their return. Plus, it's hard to be an engaging and charming "Media Darling" when you're approximating burnout from jumping at every chance that presents itself.

CLIMB encouraged us to create a new program in Women in Technology called "Thought Leadership" (and when Sandy asked me to be the Program Director, of course I said yes). The goal of this program is to help position Women in Technology as thought leaders in the community – expert resources to be consulted on technical and business issues – by showcasing their accomplishments and roles. While this was an unexpected result, it has already yielded exposure to our book contributors and the organization as a whole.

This brings us to another unexpected result of *CLIMB:* writing this book surfaced new goals in me. Because of an offer on the table to sell my publishing business, I had an open window. *CLIMB* became a conduit for my new business. When interviewing some of the women featured in the book, I heard of their desire to write their own book. My background as an author, entrepreneur and consultant organically came together in a literary consultancy, Write Advisors, LLC. You can see our website at **www.WriteAdvisors.com**. My firm helps professionals achieve the dream of publishing in the areas of business, biography and health & wellness. As I said earlier, this is the biggest reason to write a book – to start a business – and if it's a business that helps others, it's the best reason.

Being realistic, though, I need to tell you that sometimes there will be frustration and sacrifice before there is enjoyable work. And sometimes accomplishment brings new fears and uncertainty. It's all worth it because writing a book is the most powerful marketing tool you can personally create, especially if done well.

If you want to reap the benefits of creating a book, here are ten quick suggestions to do it well:

1. Understand your purpose in writing.

2. Identify your goals and make choices based on those goals.

3. Give yourself a realistic deadline.

4. Identify internal markers for success (books sold, new clients gained, etc.).

5. Try not to generate the content by yourself: assemble a support team, join a writer's critique group, or find an accountability partner.

6. Put research into your work – details matter and your audience will know.

7. Hire an editor. They'll make you look good.

8. Make your cover attractive and professional. Get others' opinions before you finalize it.

9. Be sure you know what your money is buying from a publicist.

10. If you make a mistake in the book, remember there's always a chance to correct it in a Revised Edition.

I certainly have more books to create and more changes to experience. When Vanessa Lowry asked me if I'd be interested in contributing to this book, I was thrilled. Years ago, when I was writing my first book, I had correspondence with an authority on end of life issues. We've never met, just emailed. One day, I wrote how frustrated I was, not sure if this was really what I was meant to do – write about caring for cancer patients. After all, no one else seemed to be doing it! But his two word email, "Keep Plugging!" encouraged me to finish that. Think about it: words from a stranger, helping me to create many more books, countless materials and articles.

So, maybe these words of encouragement from a stranger will help you to accomplish great things as well.

Good luck, you can do it!

See you on the other side of authorship,

Bonnie B. Daneker

Although you may be a competent individual contributor, you cannot do it all yourself... hire professionals to help you with your book.

~Bonnie B. Daneker

Chapter 4

The Art of Creating Winning Relationships Through Authoring

*Robin Hensley, The Business Development Coach for World-Class Rainmakers and President of Raising the Bar, specializes in coaching managing partners and other key law and accounting firm profitability leaders. Hensley can be found online at **www.raisingthebar.com** or on her blog at **www.theraisingthebarblog.com**.*

I've never been very interested in "how-to" books — at least not the "how to do something" kind of books. On the other hand, I've ALWAYS been inspired by how successful people achieved their success: how they overcame challenges and the wisdom they gained.

As a business development coach who works with world-class rainmakers – lawyers, CPAs and managing partners who are at the top of their game – I was constantly being approached by clients passionately suggesting that I write a book about coaching. I simply wasn't interested: my clients benefit most from one-on-one coaching in my office.

However, the "perfect storm" of events happened a few years ago, igniting my desire to write a book that would inspire me and be helpful to others.

It all started with a trip to Alabama to meet with Mr. Jack Miller, founder of Miller Hamilton, a law firm with offices in five cities that has since combined with Jones Walker. Then in his late seventies, Mr. Miller hired me as a business development coach to teach his younger lawyers, the legacy of the firm, how to embrace their expanded leadership, understand marketing and be prepared to make their own rain. While I worked with Mr. Miller's firm in Mobile each month, I spent time with his family. In the evenings, he shared his fascinating stories and opinions about how he built his firm through relationships, leadership and integrity bit by bit over nearly 30 years.

It occurred to me that if his stories and others' stories of his generation were not preserved, we'd be in danger of losing the benefit of their wisdom. The idea came to me to write a book to memorialize the great leaders of the legal community in Atlanta and possibly in Georgia. I could pass on their seasoned advice to inspire others. I started thinking about legendary lawyers I would like to interview, and the title of the book came naturally.

I'm not a writer — I'm a business development coach with 40 clients per week, including those who fly in for appointments from all over the country; and I started out as a CPA by trade. However, I thought I could "talk" a good book. I wanted to get in front of these lawyers — to learn from them as I had from Mr. Miller. Over a period of six months, I was able to interview nine of the lawyers one-on-one. Former Attorney General Griffin Bell was unable to be interviewed, but I got his personal permission to include his story.

I titled the book *Raising the Bar: Legendary Rainmakers Share Their Business Development Secrets*. The book title builds on the name recognition of my business development coaching practice, Raising the Bar. I am a strategic coach, so I make sure that whatever I do carries my brand. While my primary purpose was not as a marketing tool for my business, it has created ripples of expanding influence. I have also spent valuable one-on-one time with the cornerstones of Atlanta's legal profession. This has certainly increased my credibility and has opened doors to many opportunities.

My perfect storm got even bigger.

I am on the advisory board of the Atlanta Legal Aid Society, a non-profit that provides legal services to low-income people in Atlanta and the surrounding counties. The advisory board includes 40 lawyers and I'm one of the few non-lawyers on the board. At a meeting, representatives from the big law firms were there, pledging to dedicate hundreds of lawyers from each of their firms on a variety of projects. As a solo practitioner, I can't offer that type of help, but I wanted to do something more than just writing a check.

Since my book about legendary lawyers was already being written, the tie-in between the theme of the book and the Atlanta Legal Aid Society became clear. I decided that the majority of the profits from the $100 retail price of the book and accompanying DVD would benefit the Atlanta Legal Aid Society Endowment Fund.

So far, *Raising the Bar: Legendary Rainmakers Share Their Business Development Secrets* has raised more than $15,000 for the Atlanta Legal Aid Society.

Now, here's the nitty gritty about writing the book. This project was a huge commitment: scheduling and completing interviews, transcribing them, deciding what to include in each chapter, creating the accompanying DVD, and self-funding the publishing and printing. I decided the book would have to be a top quality, hard cover, four-color coffee table book to honor the wisdom gathered from my interviews. It needed to have substance that was equivalent to the weight of the wisdom of those featured inside. The project ended up being much more expensive than I anticipated, but because of the extra effort I put into a quality product, sales have been higher than anticipated.

As a business development coach, I teach my clients the importance of building relationships; and I practice what I teach. I had a full coaching schedule before this project began, so I needed help on the book. The process of writing, publishing and promoting was easier and the final product better because of the people who assisted me along the way.

First, I asked attorneys, judges and leaders within my network of contacts to identify the best of the best attorneys. Many of those with whom I've built relationships over the years helped me determine the perfect ten leaders to be featured, and made introductions where necessary.

I'm so grateful for their guidance in narrowing the field, and especially to the legends featured in the book for giving so generously of their time and wisdom. It was my great privilege to hear their tales of success and learn about the struggles they faced.

I also received guidance in how to capitalize on my initial investment – the book. I videotaped the interviews and included a DVD of highlighted interview segments. In addition, I've used video segments in speeches I've given since the book was released. I'll also be including edited versions of the video interviews in my blog posts. This will continue to generate interest for the book, and it will allow the wisdom from these great minds to be passed on to a wider audience. This re-purposing of content continues to be one of the ways the book is promoted.

Part of my strategy of making this book so distinctive and of high quality was to highlight the ten featured leaders in the best way, to give them a book they were proud to be part of and to create a collectible book for all who purchased it.

The book is often displayed on coffee tables. The history of how these folks made things happen in the law profession is of great interest to professionals in firms here and in other cities throughout the nation, and beyond, since many of the big firms have offices all over the world.

Many of the books sold are being given as a thank you gift. Attorneys and CPAs are giving a personally-signed copy as a thank you for a referral. They use my book as a unique gift with the added benefit of donating to a good cause. One firm plans to give signed copies of the book to their VIP clients at an upcoming conference.

I'm always looking for ways to make my clients look good and am continually building relationships. Part of my strategy behind promoting the book was to create win-win opportunities.

I focused my marketing efforts for the book on successful attorneys and CPAs. Partnering with law firms for book signings gave them the ability to plan a unique event to which they invited clients. Many of the firms who held a book signing had one or more partners highlighted in the book, and it gave them an opportunity to make their clients and prospects aware of the legends among them.

I held 23 book signings in the year following the book's release – no small task, especially when carrying on a more-than-full-time business development coaching practice.

The big initial book launch was in partnership with King & Spalding. Two of their partners are featured in the book: Judge Griffin Bell, who has since died; and Chilton Varner, the only female in the book. Another King & Spalding partner, Philip E. Holladay, Jr., is past president of the Atlanta

Legal Aid Society. King & Spalding is one of the top law firms in Atlanta and has been a strong supporter of the Atlanta Legal Aid Society for many years, so here again, this was a major opportunity to promote the book, promote the law firm, and promote Legal Aid.

I worked with Phil to coordinate the event, which included having nine of those featured in the book as guests of honor. (Judge Bell died before the book was published). King & Spalding invited their attorneys, as well as Atlanta Legal Aid board members and friends.

Because I coach accountants in addition to lawyers, BDO Seidman hosted an event and a book signing for me. I coach many partners from that firm. They network with attorneys and are very involved with them.

I approached the firm about hosting a book signing where they could invite their attorney contacts and other professionals for a networking event with a purpose. BDO coordinated all the details and I invited my clients and friends to introduce to the BDO folks. Another win for everyone, on all levels.

Mr. Frank Love and Mr. Miles Alexander, who were featured in the book, came to many events, so we often had a VIP signing books in addition to myself. Attendees were thrilled to meet an esteemed leader in the Atlanta community, and it took these networking events to the next level.

One book signing was the result of several smaller CPA firms and law firms hosting an event at my favorite home cookin' place, the Silver Skillet, a landmark "meat & three" restaurant near Georgia Tech. That was lots of fun since many of the people in the book are regulars at the Skillet, as am I.

This book signing felt like my extended family. It was fun to have libations in late afternoon after the Silver Skillet closed for the day. We had a host committee of people from several firms who invited their friends and clients – a perfect solution for smaller firms who wanted to host an event, but didn't have the capacity to hold a large number of people at their own offices. There were nearly 75 attendees – a great opportunity to mingle with members of Atlanta's law community in a relaxed setting.

Another unusual partner for two of my book signings was Saks Fifth Avenue. You know you've made some significant wardrobe investments over the years when the assistant general manager of your local Saks calls and offers to host a book signing.

One of the book signings at Saks was headed by Stephanie Casteel, of Wallace Morrison & Casteel. The resulting event was a Who's Who of women in the Bar, with 21 law firms represented... a win-win for everyone.

While book signings were a major thrust of the promotional effort for the book, I also engaged in other strategies. I hired a PR firm to get the word out in the traditional media. As a result, I was featured in an article that was published in the *Atlanta Business Chronicle* as well as in other publications.

I've built relationships with key people at the *Daily Report* over the years by contributing business development articles and partnering with them in other ways. These relationships opened the door to promoting my book to their highly-targeted readership of lawyers.

The *Daily Report* is a publication that is distributed five days a week to lawyers across the state. The metro Atlanta legal community relies on the *Daily Report* for coverage of the business of law. It is *the* publication that lawyers read. The *Daily Report* is also a great supporter of Atlanta Legal Aid.

The *Daily Report* featured excerpts from my book for 10 weeks, focusing each week on a different "legendary rainmaker" from it. This was excellent publicity for me to get to my specific target market.

I'm often asked to present as a business development expert to groups of partners and associates at firms. I use my book as the foundation of many talks, with video clips from these extraordinary rainmakers in the background. Their success reinforces the principles I teach clients every day.

My business and reputation has benefitted in many ways from the expanded exposure through publishing *Raising the Bar.* Many of those featured in the book were connected to firms for whom I coach managing partners, practice team leaders or super rainmakers.

The book opened doors to new firms, as well. For example, I didn't know Governor Carl Sanders and hadn't been coaching anyone at his firm, Troutman Sanders. Asking to feature their founder in my book was an excellent way to get to know the key people within the firm, along with their goals and philosophies.

On a personal note, just being in the presence of these successful people while doing their interviews was well worth the effort for me. Miles Alexander said, "Lawyers are most effective when they listen. Little is learned while talking." I learned a great deal from listening to these legends of law; and I am now able to share their information.

Since then, I've also created several eBooks focused on specific topics for my target market of attorneys and CPAs. Most recently, I partnered with renowned attorney, John C. Yates, of Morris, Manning & Martin, LLP, and launched *Super Rainmaking: 10 Secrets To Raising the Bar In Your Professional Practice.*

John shared his secrets for increasing effectiveness in business development efforts. I provided a coaching message at the end of each chapter. Profits from the sale of this eBook support John's favorite cause, CURE Childhood Cancer.

I have people ask me about how I was able to write, publish and promote a book while heading my busy coaching practice. Motivation is fueled by inspiration. I was completely inspired by learning from these people who changed the course of history in Atlanta and beyond.

The key is to have a plan (including a budget and timeline), determine your strengths, and find people to help in the areas where you are weak. Create a list of duties and determine who's going to do the items on your list.

After you commit to writing a book, don't stop. Not many people finish and it really does take a lot of dedication, especially if it's not your full-time effort. I felt responsible to the leaders featured in the book and to my pledge to raise money for Atlanta Legal Aid. I managed to complete the book in just over a year, and I had plenty of help. There are two pages in the book of people I acknowledge who helped me bring it to publication.

As Bernie Fuchs says, "Commitment is a line you must cross... it is the difference between dreaming and doing."

After you commit to writing a book, don't stop. Motivation is fueled by inspiration.

~*Robin Hensley*

Chapter 5

Attracting Clients After a Career Shift

Vanessa Lowry is an author, radio host, speaker, graphic designer and marketing consultant. She leverages nearly 30 years of design and marketing expertise to support book authors who are self publishing. **www.connect4leverage.com**

My first book, *30 Days of Gratitude*, was born out of despair. I made a difficult decision to close my business, Profits in Progress, in February of 2009. Enormous amounts of energy and my savings had been invested into the business for nearly six years. At this same time, the economy was sliding into the largest recession since the Great Depression. Closing this business was heartbreaking and I found it very difficult to decide in which new direction to move.

Soon after closing Profits in Progress, one of my long-time graphic design clients hired me to design the cover for his soon to be published book, *Uprooting Anger*. Charlie and I shared a dynamic collaboration as we created a cover that illustrated the content of his book, would attract his target reader and supported his vision. As a result of this project, I decided a target niche of future clients would be authors who are self publishing.

Even as I began to venture into the self publishing arena, I felt I needed to publish my own book so I could understand the process more completely. I talked with authors, reviewed many books written by entrepreneurs and made connections with others who work in the field of book publishing. I began to see ways to develop a book that didn't require a huge commitment of time or extensive experience as a writer.

The second part of this equation was that I devoted a lot of time to prayer, meditation and writing in my journal as ways to release my feelings of failure. I wrote through months of depression. The teachings of Joel Osteen, Byron Katie and Abraham-Hicks were particularly beneficial in helping me examine my thoughts and understand that I had a choice of what thoughts to focus upon. Scripture and inspirational quotes were a healing balm to what felt like a gaping wound in my spirit.

During these months, I more clearly understood that focusing on the things in my life that I appreciated helped me inch forward. Listing reasons to be happy for even very small things made it possible to relax into a place of peace, even during this time of uncertainty. I used a mala (a string of 108 prayer beads) and as I touched each bead I said a prayer of thanks for someone or something in my life. Sometimes it was an affirmation that I said over and over with each bead.

My friend Wendy Watkins began posting an update on Facebook of things she appreciated about her life that day starting with a specific letter of the alphabet. She encouraged others to post their gratitude with each letter as well. Through the next few weeks, Wendy went from A-Z and I saw how powerful having a very specific exercise to use as a gratitude spark was for finding joy in the moment.

I thought a book of 30 short exercises would not only be easy to create, but would be a powerful book for my own practice in noticing where I had abundance and for what I was grateful. It would be a book that a reader could use as a daily point of inspiration and a way of looking through new eyes of appreciation at their life.

I reached out to two girlfriends – Robin Kirby and Carolyn Buttram, also fellow entrepreneurs – to see if they would be willing to collaborate with me on this book. They both immediately resonated with the concept and agreed to help write and promote the book through their networks of friends and contacts. From the beginning, we agreed to make the book a free download so more people would benefit from the practice of gratitude. (You can download the free book at **www.daysofgratitude.com**.)

A key reason I asked Robin and Carolyn to be part of this project is that we each believe that once the energy of gratitude begins to roll forward, it has far reaching effects beyond any one individual's control. A statement on the first page of our book reads, "As you express gratitude, it spirals back to you... expanded into multiple forms."

As we started this process, we said, "Wouldn't it be nice to have the book launched for people to use for 30 days in November, the month of Thanksgiving?"

Many people find areas of their life where they experience "flow." This book was definitely an example of that principle in action. I approached Robin and Carolyn the first week of October 2009 about collaborating with me. We had the book complete and available for download on our new website by October 29th. It was less than three weeks from conception to completion, including custom photography by Carolyn for the cover. She also set up our website at **www.daysofgratitude.com**.

The day after emails were sent about the book launch, I got a call from the Atlanta Theosophical Society. They wanted to book "The Gratitude Girls" for our first speaking engagement. That presentation was videotaped and is still posted on the PBS Forum website at this link: **http://forum-network.org/lecture/gratitude-girls-30-days-gratitude.**

In the two years since that book launched, I have made presentations or been a radio guest on the topic of gratitude an average of every other month. Within a week of our launch, the book was downloaded from all over the world including New Zealand, Croatia, Thailand, Spain, South Africa and more. Gratitude Girl, Robin Kirby, created our Days of Gratitude Facebook page and posts an inspirational quote daily. At the time of this book's printing, we have nearly 1,700 fans on that page.

We have hosted Gratitude Parties and Gratitude Meet-ups to sell printed copies of our book, as well as a way to connect face-to-face with others who resonate with the energetic power of gratitude. Companies have purchased our book in bulk as a giveaway for employees and as client gifts.

Since *30 Days of Gratitude* was released, I find that many clients hire me because they feel our outlook on life matches.

Sherri Lane is a client who contacted me after first connecting through the Days of Gratitude Facebook page and blog. While Sherri was still writing her manuscript, she called me to discuss her book cover. Writing can be a very solitary practice and authors sometimes get bogged down in the process of writing and re-writing. Sherri understood the power of visualization and wanted to have a compelling cover to encourage her as she continued to write. The book cover was a tangible way to help her envision the book as completed.

Sherri is an author who seeks to bring out the best in others by recognizing the good in the world. She felt it was important to have a designer who shared her understanding of the energetic world. I was thrilled to play a part in her publishing journey. Her book, *Setting God Free*, is now available at **www.sherrilane.com**, as well as Amazon, Barnes & Noble on-line and in many bookstores.

In August of 2010 I began gathering collaborators for my next book, *Improv to Improve Your Business*. I took an improv course in 2008 and saw how the principles helped me listen more effectively and increase my creativity as I worked with clients. I approached Brent Brooks who taught the improv course and he helped me connect with other students who had taken his classes. I also approached my network of contacts and found others who had taken improv and felt this would be a good way to market their businesses.

The Q&A area of LinkedIn is a great resource for connection and gathering information. I posted a question asking business professionals who had taken improv classes to share how it helped them in business. From those responses, another co-author joined our book project. Many other respondents gave permission for their answers to be printed in the book's chapter titled "Other Contributors."

Since the release of *Improv to Improve Your Business*, each co-author has benefitted from their fellow co-authors promoting the book. We made a radio appearance on Atlanta Business Radio with the entire show dedicated to our book topic. Five of our nine co-authors were available for that interview.

I have been a featured speaker at business organizations on the topic of "Improv to Improve Your Business." Many of my "Improv" co-authors have appeared as experts on this topic in a variety of business opportunities.

Sharing my expertise by speaking to business and civic groups is a key way that I connect with new clients. Having published my own books lends credibility to my presentations. In addition to being a speaker on gratitude and improv topics, I often give presentations to authors and aspiring authors on book publishing, marketing and design.

I was recently a featured speaker for a publishing conference hosted at Kennesaw State University and organized by the Master of Arts in Professional Writing graduate program and the Georgia Writers Association. My presentation topic was "30 Ways to Market Your Book Before and After Publishing." The information from the handout given to participants on that day is included in this book, beginning on page 115.

Many of the authors I work with are business professionals, but may not have worked with a graphic designer in their business role. Having some initial ideas, sharing examples that appeal to you and being open to creative collaboration can generate a powerful completed book and an enjoyable publishing journey. I've included tips on working with a graphic designer on page 107.

There are many benefits of collaboration. When I share an idea and you share an idea, we each have two ideas. Often, an even better idea is sparked from the combination of two or more ideas. I found an example that Stephen Covey gives in his best-selling book *The 7 Habits of Highly Effective People* to be particularly helpful. He shares the example of a triangle to describe a "Third Alternative." The third alternative is achieved by looking for creative opportunities which are win-win and synergistic.

Think of collaboration as a triangle. Your idea is the bottom point on one side of the triangle and my idea is the bottom point on the same plane, but on the opposite side. The new idea is not only the intersection of our original ideas, but on a higher plane that the two base points. The third point is at a higher point that wouldn't have been possible without the two initial bottom points coming together in a "third alternative."

In successful collaboration, the work is shared and the time needed to accomplish a task is reduced. This book, *Publishing as a Marketing Strategy,* is an example of collaboration around a particular topic. The co-authors shared their experiences and ideas. We all benefit from the variety of perspectives and experiences. The entire project was completed in less than six months and is a marketing opportunity for each co-author to be exposed to potential clients that might not have found them another way.

In addition to my own experience as an author, skill as a graphic designer and expertise as a marketing consultant, I've accumulated many contacts to assist authors every step of the way. Some of these include writing coaches, editors, print-on-demand vendors, video production companies, PR firms, web designers, and virtual assistants.

Over the past year, I've collaborated with my client and friend Tim Morrison. He is the host of *Write Here, Write Now*, a weekly radio show airing on BusinessRadioX.com. Tim invited me to guest host his show once a month and I've found it an ideal way to highlight my clients and their books. I also get the opportunity to meet authors with whom I haven't worked and hear their journey of writing and publishing. On pages 123-126, I've listed several interviews from *Write Here, Write Now* that might be particularly helpful to you in writing and getting your book published. Get ideas for the type of book you may want to write by listening to the mp3 recordings of past shows. You can access show archives at **www.writeherewritenow. businessradiox.com.**

I'm excited about the multi-media project I'm launching in 2012. It is a new type of collaboration for me on the topic of "Art as Worship." I'll host a weekly radio show interviewing artists who feel their creative expressions are an extension of their spiritual practice. Content from the interviews will be used to create a book exploring this topic from the perspective of many faiths, artistic media and methods of expression. If you know an artist who might like to be interviewed, please email me at **vlowry@gmail.com.** Find out more this project at **www.artasworship.net.**

I love books. I love the ideas I get, the things I learn and the adventures upon which I embark just by reading a good book. Books can be a gateway to healing, gaining perspective and expanding my understanding of the world. I find that all types and genres of books have the power to spark a new idea or build on an idea that needs expanding.

There are many types of books that can serve as a marketing tool for your business. The other chapters of this book highlight a variety of book types and publishing journeys.

Here are examples from a few of my clients:

A "tips" book can be accomplished very quickly and requires a minimum amount of text. An example is *Basic Writing Tips for Emerging Writers: A Manual to Help You Focus and to Improve Your Writing from the Start*, a pocket-size book published by writing coach Tim Morrison. This 110-page book is filled with short tips and resources. The colors on the cover are the same as the logo for Tim's company, Write Choice Services. His logo includes a graphic of a hand holding a pen, so I duplicated that graphic and used it to visually identify each new tip. The starburst from his logo is used as section dividers. The entire book supports the branding of Write Choice Services from the content through the appearance. Tim's radio show, *Write Here, Write Now* is also prominently featured on the cover and in a chapter of the book. **www.writechoiceservices.com**

Laura Biering's book, *The RiskADay Journal,* is another example of publishing a book quickly since much of the material was already created and just needed to be collected and organized. Laura wrote of personal experiences and those of her clients to explain the power of the exercises, charts and diagrams she already used with her coaching clients. She added journal pages to encourage the reader to participate in a 28-day journey of taking a risk every day. **www.theriskadayjournal.com**

Other clients find they are called to write a book that is more substantive. Writing this type of book is a longer process and gives prospective clients a behind-the-scenes view into the unique expertise of that author. Charlie Cummins' book *Uprooting Anger* shares his personal experiences with anger combined with methods he uses as a therapist to help his clients heal from the ravages of anger. His story resonates with those who struggle from the effects of anger because he overcame the challenge himself. As a result of publishing this book, he has changed the branding of his clinical practice to focus upon the niche of angry men. **www.angrymancounseling.com**

Myra McElhaney has published books to highlight her writing and to promote her keynote speeches and workshops. *Mama Always Says* is a collection of quotes from many mamas. *Musings on Major and Minor Matters That May or May Not Matter* shows the humor Myra brings to joyful moments in her life as well as difficult ones. **www.myramcelhaney.com**

It thrills me to collaborate with clients to get their ideas out into the world in a powerful way. The opportunity to launch my own ideas with assistance and support from others has become a joy-filled journey. Advances in technology make it easier and cheaper than ever before to transfer your knowledge, expertise and imagination onto the printed page and publish your own book. As a result, new clients, opportunities and collaborations will present themselves in ways you never expected.

*In successful collaboration,
"third alternatives" present
themselves, work is shared
and time needed to accomplish
a task is reduced.*

~Vanessa Lowry

Chapter 6

Leverage: The Power to Build Your Brand and Your Professional Platform

Anita R. Paul, *Author's Coach, Writer Extradonaire, and President of The Write Image, mentors corporate professionals and successful entrepreneurs to upsell their expertise by becoming a published author, and then to leverage their book for their success. She can be reached at **www.writeyourlife.net** and at **www.thewriteimage.net**.*

Indoor rock climbing has become a ferociously popular and competitive sport for moderately adventurous souls. That is to say, those of us too chicken to climb an actual rock – one the likes of Half Dome in Yosemite National Park or The Ophir Wall in Telluride, Colorado – often settle for gearing up with harness and ropes, along with a trusted partner, and knuckling a few climbing holds in the relative safety of a gym in hopes of reaching the top, cascading down gracefully, and then grabbing a beer afterwards.

One thing I've learned from my indoor rock climbing experiences – and trust me, there haven't been many – is the power of leverage. When you're on the wall sweating and reaching for the top, you are determined to use every nook and cranny to dig in a toe, finger, elbow, or knee to ensure you don't fall and that you reach your goal: the top. That's leverage. We all want to reach the top, don't we? We want to be at the top of our game and at the top of our industry. It takes talent, teamwork, and yes, leverage, to do that.

Financially speaking, leverage is a technique to multiply gains and losses. In the 1300s, the English used the word as an equivalent to "lighten or lift." In the general business sense, leverage means to influence people, events, or decisions; to sway; to exert power or influence. That is exactly what becoming an author has done for me and for countless other entrepreneurs and professionals. And that's what it can do for you, too.

A Lesson Learned

In 2002, I published my first book, *Take the Mystery Out of Marketing.* The content of the e-book explained the intricacies of marketing in a very simple format, helping micro businesses and non-profits make sense of the terminology, benefits, differences, and advantages of various marketing tools and strategies. For years, as the president of The Write Image, I developed marketing plans and public relations programs for organizations that took my word as gold. They saw my plans as brilliant, creative, and flawless. Why did they believe in me? One reason is that I had positioned myself as an expert and an authority based on my industry experience. And then, of course, I had a book to prove my worth.

Problem was, I didn't publicize the book. That's right, the publicist didn't publicize. Oh sure, I told my circle of influence that I had written an e-book, some of them bought it, others shared the news with their colleagues and they purchased it. But it didn't sell in great number and it didn't grow wings. Worse yet, I didn't leverage it to get to the top. Instead, I kept the news of this rich little guide closely held within the confines of my comfort zone ... and life went on.

Fast forward to 2010 when I was in the throes of redefining my 13-year-old communications company. Over the years, I had worked with numerous authors to help publicize their books, brand them as experts, and to even manage the production of their next book. All of them were professionals in their own right. These authors had written how-to books, memoirs, and autobiographies detailing their experiences, knowledge, and expertise. For years, I had been attracting these talented authors, professionals, and entrepreneurs as clients. They wanted my expertise in helping them publicize their book and themselves. Sometimes you just can't ignore where life is leading you, so I revamped The Write Image to focus on coaching and mentoring corporate professionals and entrepreneurs who wanted to become authors and those who had already written books. More importantly, I began coaching these already successful people to leverage their knowledge, in book form, and to upsell their expertise.

How could a marketing communications guru shift to becoming a self publishing author's coach and mentor? In addition to my years of experience in marketing and public relations, I needed something more to stand on. In essence, I needed some leverage. I had to walk the talk that I was sharing with my clients; I needed a new book. So I quickly went about the business of planning, writing, and publishing my second book, *Write Your Life: Create Your Ideal Life and the Book You've Been Wanting to Write.*

This book evolved almost effortlessly as a journal to help aspiring authors utilize journaling as a framework for their memoir, autobiography, or how-to book. Journaling has long been a refuge for me, and I wanted to share the gift of journaling with an audience that needed a foundation for creating their lever; a unique product they would eventually use to leverage their success.

The Road You Choose

Over the last few decades, self publishing has slowly gained a more respectable reputation. Still not on par with traditional publishing, the self publishing industry has, in my opinion, compensated for its lack of prestige and respect by upping the ante on quality. With so many people having so much to say about what they know or have experienced, and with so many readers hungry for accurate information and a good story, the self publishing marketplace had to meet the demand for higher quality. People want to read not only well-written books, but also professionally produced ones.

I chose the road of self publishing for two reasons: 1) because I wanted to get the book produced quickly; and 2) because I wanted to see how the self publishing industry had changed since my first book was published. I needed this information and the experience so I could share it with my clients. Early on, I knew this would have to be a team effort. I had the writing part down pat, but what about the rest?

Throughout the process, my team developed: First the tight circle of influence who would review the manuscript and offer constructive comments. These reviewers were carefully selected to reflect the ideal readers for my book, and those who would give me honest feedback. Then, there were colleagues who recommended the divine right people to help mold the manuscript into an easy-to-read product. The first came in the form of a professional editor – a woman who helped me realize that being a great writer didn't make me a master of the English language! Then, there were the seemingly accidental – but actually, divinely guided – mentions of a printer, a publicist, a layout specialist, a graphic designer, a web developer, and so on. Before I knew it, my power team had formed.

I started talking about my book before it was complete, and people would recommend a colleague they thought I should meet or an event they thought I should attend. Almost overnight, it seemed as if a flood of opportunities opened up for me – speaking engagements, invitations to join networking groups, opportunities to become a guest blogger, connections with strategic partners. All the right people continued to be drawn to me.

Know What You Want

During the process of writing the book, my mind was flooded with creative ideas for how to leverage it. I was developing a new business model and platform for The Write Image. I was beginning to brand myself as the go-to person for effectively writing a book, connecting with the resources to produce a quality self published book, and leveraging that book for long-term success. My consciousness shifted to attract even more people, information, and opportunities that would be a good fit for this new business model. Making the decision to write the book was the fuel that got the fire started. I knew what I wanted, and while the plan wasn't completely worked out, I began moving in the direction of my vision.

From the very start, the book was less about selling a stack of bound paper with my name on a pretty cover, and more about leveraging my wealth of information to establish myself as an authority. I wanted to capitalize on my gift and skill as a writer, my industry contacts, and my experience as a marketing and public relations expert. Combining those capabilities was the perfect storm, so to speak, for developing the new brand for The Write Image. In essence, I was recreating my platform.

Every author, no matter your background, interests, or experience, needs a platform. This is what you stand for, what you want (for yourself and for others), what you know, and what you're passionate about. It is your motivation for continuing in the direction in which you're moving, especially when things get difficult and suddenly don't make sense and you wonder, "What am I doing and what have I gotten myself into?" The answer can be found in your platform. As I reinvented my company, helping authors create quality books and motivating non-writers to tell their stories became my platform.

I saw *Write Your Life* as a resource, a tool, an information product that spoke volumes of my expertise and my ability to teach others to craft a quality book. But why stop there? From the one book, I began to develop several other information products. After all, we are in the golden age of information. People all over the world have ideas. Oftentimes, all they need is the information to know how to do what they want to do, and they're off to create the next great thing. I wanted to be a part of that revolution. I saw information products as a key to helping others give life to their vision, and possibly to further their platform.

So *Write Your Life*, the book, became Write Your Life, the program. Marketing the book was an extension of marketing the overall program. I created several tools to market the book, the program, and myself as an expert:

- A blog called "Write Your Life."
- An ezine called "Book Your Success."
- A social media presence on Facebook, Twitter, and LinkedIn.
- A suite of information products including PDFs, mp3s, and CDs.
- Several signature talks to highlight my expertise.
- A speaker sheet to demonstrate my capabilities and experience in front of an audience.

- A mastermind group called Upsell Your Expertise for authors and aspiring authors wishing to leverage their books.

- The F.L.O.W. Retreat to help journalers, writers, and authors tap into their creative gifts. (F.L.O.W. is my signature retreat, heavily focused on teaching people to Follow Life's Overtures in Wisdom.).

- Upsell U., a curriculum for women professionals and entrepreneurs to help them identify their personal and professional strengths, and develop ways to communicate, demonstrate, capitalize on, and profit from them.

Your book could be the perfect complement to your already rich offering of products and services, or it could be the beginning of a completely new aspect of your business or career. Never see your book as a "one hit wonder." If you really want to leverage your book and use it to support your platform, you must expand your view of what the book represents. Get creative about how you can leverage your book to realize your vision. Consider as many mediums as possible — social media, in-person (speaking, networking, etc.), telephone, recordings (video and audio), print, direct mail, email, fax. The sky is the limit!

Become A Magnet

As I developed the various branches of the Write Your Life Program, I felt that I was flowing seamlessly in my long-held belief that when you move in the direction of your vision and your dream, all sorts of opportunities are drawn to you. I became a magnet for my desires, and every time I said yes, more opportunities appeared.

Mind you, I said yes a few too many times, and realized that I had accepted an opportunity that either was not for me at that time or would not lead me to where I ultimately wanted to be, so I had to back out of it. I did this twice within a six-month period. The decision to withdraw was made through quiet, careful, honest evaluation. Would I feel better continuing down the road of the commitment I had made, or would I feel relieved at letting go, apologizing to those to whom I had made the commitment, and moving forward with an open slot for another, more appropriate opportunity to insert itself? In both instances I chose the latter, and sure enough, another opportunity came about almost immediately.

The book, and the resulting program I created around it, gave me the clarity, confidence, and credibility to attract even more of the right opportunities. All of this was the leverage I needed to establish and build upon my new business model.

Measures Of Success

The measure of success for *Write Your Life* was never about book sales alone, although every author wants to sell books. My clients and the audiences to whom I speak often glance at me with raised eyebrows when I suggest that book sales should not be the primary nor the sole measure of the success of your book. Honestly, if you don't have a grander platform than selling books, you're probably not my ideal client. It has taken some time for me to confidently say that, but let me explain why this is.

Every one of us has a gift and a calling. For every moment that you are not walking in your calling, you are not living the purpose for which you were created. For every second that you are not practicing your gift, you are missing out on the phenomenal blessings that you have been placed in this earth at this time to experience. Trust me, your calling is greater than selling a million books.

Your calling could be to raise funds to build wells in Africa. Your gift could be teaching blind children to play the violin. Perhaps you were placed on this earth to discover a cure for lupus or to invent a gadget to make life easier for those with arthritis. Maybe your intangible calling is to uplift downtrodden souls or to encourage and inspire inner-city residents to take ownership of their communities. Maybe you're a connector, and your life is all about connecting people with the resources they need to succeed. Whatever your calling or your gift, you have a story. You know your stuff. You have information that others need to know. Sharing your knowledge in the form of a book is one of the best ways to express your calling and to influence others. But how can you tell if your book achieves the goals you intend?

The measures of success for me and my book were first internal:

- Did I feel confident and capable moving in this new direction?

- Was I allowing my authentic self to evolve through this process?

- Was I adding value to the lives of others?

- Was I following life's overtures in wisdom?

- Was I utilizing my gifts and my calling?

Other measures of success were more business focused:

- Could I leverage the book to upsell my expertise?

- Would the book complement my new business model?

- Could I repurpose the content of the book in other formats?

- Could what I was building stand without me as a primary pillar?

- Could I leverage the book to build my brand and my professional platform?

My answers to each of these questions, and so many others, had to be undeniably yes. You see, *Write Your Life* is really my attempt to communicate that life is better when you RIGHT Your Life. Live your dreams. Accomplish your goals. Experience your vision. It's all possible when you leverage your knowledge and your expertise.

So what happens when your book has succeeded in being the leverage you needed to get to the top? What happens when you achieve your grand dream? In the words of self-made billionaire media mogul, Oprah Winfrey, "Get a bigger dream!"

*Every author needs a platform.
This is what you stand for,
what you want (for yourself
and for others), what you
know, and what you're
passionate about.*

~Anita R. Paul

Chapter 7

Choosing Your Best Path to Publishing

*Ahmad Meradji is the President and CEO of BookLogix Publishing Services. He specializes in educating authors on, and guiding them through, the Self Publishing process. He can be reached through **www.booklogix.com** or at 770-346-9979.*

So, you've decided that writing a book is a smart choice to help you promote your business. Great, time to start writing! But there's more to consider than just writing the book. You'll have to decide how to publish it as well. You have two paths to choose from – traditional publishing or self publishing.

Traditional Publishing vs. Self Publishing

In *traditional publishing*, the author submits his or her manuscript to any number of publishing houses for consideration. The manuscript is reviewed by an editor, who either decides it is right for the house and makes plans to publish it, or rejects it. If the publishing house decides to buy the book, it purchases the rights from the writer and pays the writer an advance on future royalties. Royalties are payouts, based on the profit of each book sold. For example, if the cost of the book was $5 to make and distribute, and they sold it for $14.99, you would get a percentage of the $9.99 difference. The publishing house covers the costs of design and layout of the book, prints a number of copies it expects to sell, and then markets the book and oversees distribution. They also oversee any syndication and translation processes.

Many authors first try submitting to traditional publishers because they're hoping for that big advancement check. (A 2009 article in the *New York Times* said the average advancement was roughly $30,000.) Or they don't want the responsibility of overseeing the printing or marketing of their book. But these days it's getting harder and harder for authors to get their manuscript picked up by a traditional publisher. Traditional publishers seem to be taking fewer risks, instead choosing to focus on proven, best-selling authors. Mentally prepare yourself for rejection. Margaret Mitchell's *Gone with the Wind* was rejected 38 times and J.K. Rowling's original work was turned down by 12 publishers.

In *self publishing*, the author manages the entire publishing process of their book. A self publishing author also funds the publishing process. Once the manuscript is written, the author selects an editor, a graphic designer, illustrator, printer, marketing/promotion service, and distributor. Several factors have contributed to the growth of self publishing in the past few years, including advances in printing technology, the growth of the internet, alternative publishing methods such as eBook publishing, and many outlets for online distribution. Control over what happens to their book, keeping the rights to their work, higher royalty amounts per copy sold and a growing number of distribution options available are making self publishing a more attractive choice to a growing number of authors. Anywhere from 8,000 to 11,000 new publishers enter the field every year. Most of those are self publishers.

In the past few years, the industry has seen giant leaps in the number of "non-traditional" books published.

Non-traditional titles include on-demand titles and titles by self publishers. 78% of titles come from a small press or self publisher. According to R.R. Bowker, the number of non-traditional titles published in 2010 rose 169%; since 2002, the production of non-traditional books has increased 8,460%.

Mindset Shift

Authors who decide to self publish need to undergo a shift in their thinking. They are no longer a *writer* or an *author*, they are now a *publisher*. They now have to make business decisions related to the book, such as defining the target audience, selecting a cover that "sells" the book, pricing the book correctly, planning marketing strategies, working with distributors or retailers, and more.

Help and Guidance for Self Publishers

The author can select and manage all of the service providers needed themselves, or can enlist the services of one of a growing number of publishing support providers. A publishing support provider manages the publishing process with the author's input, and selects the designers, editors, printers and others needed to complete the publishing process. When using a publishing support provider, the author is still considered to be the publisher.

There are a number of companies out there offering to help you publish your book, but it's important to consider what they're offering. Providers offer a range of services and price options. An author who plans to self publish needs to research these providers to learn more about how their rights to their work could be affected, how much input and control they will have in each step of the publishing process, and most importantly, what, if any, contract does the provider have? Always look for a contract that you can cancel any time, and be wary of any contract that seeks to have you sign over the rights to your book or any future works you write. Whenever possible consult a lawyer to be sure you and your work are protected.

Steps of Publishing

The steps of the publishing process can seem overwhelming, causing many writers to not want to choose the self publishing path. But when you break the process down into steps, it's not as scary as it seems.

WRITING

Authors think that the majority of their work in publishing their book will be in actually writing the book. And on average, it takes about 475 hours to write a novel, 725 hours to write a nonfiction book. But in the publishing process, the marketing of the book, which is on-going in order to keep sales of the book going, ends up being the most important factor. How will anyone read what you've written if they don't know about your book to begin with?

EDITING AND "DOCTORING"

The goal of the editing process is to make your book a better version of itself. The process can vary based on the level of editing your book requires. Your publishing support provider can recommend the proper level of editing needed for your manuscript. When selecting an editor, ask if they will edit your manuscript on paper or in the electronic file. Some editors still edit on paper. Also be sure that the editor will not make permanent changes to your manuscript without your consent. Check to see if they will use a feature such as Microsoft Word's "Track Changes" so that you have the option to accept or reject the editor's suggested changes.

COVER DESIGN/INTERIOR TEXT FORMATTING

The look of your book is as important as the story inside, if not more! Your book's cover and interior design must be clean and eye-catching. 75% of booksellers surveyed said the look and design of the book cover is the most important component of selling a book. On average a bookstore shopper will spend just 8 seconds looking at the front cover and 15 seconds on the back!

Be sure that any photos used on the cover or inside your book are high resolution photos. New self publishers sometimes wonder why photos on their printed pages don't look as good as they did on a computer screen, and this is due to the resolution of the photos.

BOOK REGISTRATIONS

Your book will need some identification to help retailers and libraries catalog and track your book, as well as distinguish between editions. Time for some alphabet soup!

ISBN: INTERNATIONAL STANDARD BOOK NUMBER

The ISBN is a number that identifies your book for retailers. It is used to create the Barcode you see on the back of books, and is also listed on the book's Copyright page. An ISBN must be unique to each edition of your book - so the hardcover and paperback must have different numbers, and if you have an eBook, that will have its own number as well, sometimes referred to as an eISBN. If you plan to sell your book on your website or at events such as book fairs, you won't need an ISBN. An ISBN is needed if you want to work with retailers (online and brick-and-mortar) and distributors.

If you make changes to your book at any point, other than correcting minor typos, you will need to get a new

ISBN for the book. I often recommend that self publishers wait to get an ISBN for their book until they've done a small first printing run, so that if they decide to make a number of changes, or change anything major such as doing a new cover, then they will not need to purchase a new ISBN.

The owner of the ISBN on a book has the rights to sell the book. If you want to control all the selling of your book, and work directly with retailers and distributors, then you'll want to purchase an ISBN that is registered to you. If you'd like for your publishing support provider to handle sales of your book, you can purchase one of their ISBNs. If you purchase your own ISBN, you should only purchase it through Bowker, the agency in the U.S. that handles ISBN registration. You can purchase through them by visiting **www.myidentifiers.com**.

BARCODE

The barcode on your book's cover is scanned by retailers when selling an inventorying your book. The barcode contains your books ISBN and price. Barcodes can be purchased at the time you purchase an ISBN, or your publishing support provider may create one for you as part of their services.

LCCN: LIBRARY OF CONGRESS CONTROL NUMBER

The Library of Congress Control Number (LCCN) is a unique record assigned to a title by the Library of Congress. The number is used by libraries to identify books in their cataloged collections. The number should be placed on a book's Copyright page.

COPYRIGHT

Copyright protects works from infringement under U.S. law. Holding the copyright to a work gives the holder the right to reproduce, distribute, perform/display or create derivatives of a work. Copyright protection lasts for 70 years after the author's death.

You don't have to file formal copyright registration to protect your work. When writing your manuscript, put the word 'Copyright' or the © with the year and your full name on the manuscript. This grants the manuscript copyright protection without having to file it with the Copyright office. You may want to do this on every page of the manuscript, using the header/footer feature, to ensure that pages are protected if they are somehow separated when you're submitting or sharing your manuscript.

You may have heard that your manuscript will have copyright protection if you mail yourself a copy and do not open it. It's sometimes called the "poor man's copyright." But the U.S. Copyright Office says there is no provision in the copyright law regarding this type of protection, and that it is not a substitute for filing a copyright registration.

You will want to file a formal copyright registration if you anticipate needing to protect your book in a legal case of some kind, such as filing an infringement lawsuit. Be aware that any information you provide to the U.S. Copyright office will become public record and will be visible on the internet. I encourage authors to register a finished copy of their book to the Copyright Office instead of just the manuscript. The manuscript will undergo editing, layout, etc. and will look nothing like that original form once published.

Remember that not everything is protected by filing copyright registration for your book. Titles and names of characters are not protected. If you wish to protect the title of your book, you can file a Trademark application.

BOOK PRINTING

The development of print on-demand technology has enhanced the abilities of an author to publish their own book – from the ability to get a single printed and bound proof copy to ordering as few as 1 book at a time, or having book orders filled as they come in.

There are many choices for a self publisher to consider when it comes to printing their book:

- what cover type (hardcover, softcover)
- binding (perfect paperback, saddle stitching)
- text page stock and protective coating (lamination, U.V. coating)
- inside pages: color or black & white
- how many to print
- cost per book

Digital vs. Offset Printing

In digital printing, ink or toner forms a thin layer on the surface of the paper. Digital printing allows for variable text and images. Why print in digital format? In addition to fast turn-around times and the ability to easily print new copies when a file is changed, digital printing has made self publishing much more profitable for self publishers, as they can print as few copies as they would like at a time, eliminating over-ordering.

Offset printing uses plates and ink to transfer text and images onto paper. The ink is absorbed into the paper. When more than one color is needed, a separate plate for each ink is used. Offset printing becomes cost-effective when high quantities of a book are ordered, so a self publisher might utilize both digital and offset printing in the life cycle of the book.

HOW MANY COPIES?

So many self publishers who had little or no guidance their first time around end up with boxes and boxes of books that they cannot sell. I always recommend that you print no more than 25 copies in the first run. These copies should be given to peers and reviewers so that the author can get feedback. In my experience, about 95% of authors find things they want to change, whether it's punctuation/grammar issues or flaws in their plot, etc. If you print 300 books and then find things that need to be corrected, what happens to those "bad" books? And do you have enough left in your budget to print more?

Another reason not to print lots of extra books: the average number of copies sold per title from a Print On-Demand company with 10,000 different titles was just 75 books.

Print On-Demand vs. Ship On-Demand

Print On-Demand (POD) = Sell, Print, Ship

Ship On-Demand (SOD) = Print, Inventory (storage), Sell, Ship

With print on-demand, the self publisher can list their book for sale without having to print copies ahead of time. Then as an order comes in, a book is printed and shipped by the publishing support provider. With POD there is no need to store books in the basement or garage. With SOD, a self publisher can order a desired quantity of their books, hold onto them, and then ship them out after an order comes in.

EBOOK CONVERSION

The publishing industry has seen an explosion in the eBooks market. Amazon reported in 2011 that for every

100 print books sold, 105 Kindle books are sold. A *USA Today* article from February 2011 reported that 20 million people read eBooks in 2010. For the first two months of 2011, a survey of 16 publishers showed e-book sales were up 169.4%, to $164.1 million, which equaled the sales of trade paperback books for the two-month period.

So What Is An eBook?

eBooks are digital editions of print books. They are set in a re-flowable format, to allow compatibility with a variety of eReader devices and the ability of the user to change font size as desired. eBooks are not meant to look exactly like the print edition - fancy fonts may be converted to standard styles, and images may be resized to fit screen size. eBooks also do not have page numbers, as they will vary in length from the print edition, so instead of page numbers in the Table of Contents, electronic links are used.

There are two major file types for eBooks: ePub and Mobi. ePub is a universal file type that works on the Nook from Barnes & Noble and Apple's iPad. Mobi works on Amazon's Kindle and the Mobipocket reader.

FILE CONVERSION

Conversion to eBook format usually starts with a Microsoft Word or PDF source file. Some sites assist authors in doing their own conversion, including Amazon's Kindle Direct Publishing and Smashwords. But professional conversion may be needed if your book has lots of images or complex formatting, or in order to sell your eBook with other retailers.

DRM: DIGITAL RIGHTS MANAGEMENT

One concern with selling a book in an electronic file format is that an eBook is more vulnerable to piracy. DRM, or Digital Rights Management, protects an eBook file from being copied once it is purchased from a retailer. Not all eBook files have DRM on them after conversion. DRM can be added on when a file is uploaded to one of the major retailers, such as Amazon or Barnes & Noble.

WHY PUBLISH IN EBOOK FORMAT?

eBooks are not only easy to distribute, they are more cost effective and allow for higher revenue potential. Once a file is converted, there's no additional manufacturing cost or shipping costs. Royalty percentages are high (60%, 65%, 70%) as long as an eBook's price falls within a certain range that meets retailers' requirements. If you've had eBook conversion that provides you with the 2 major file formats, your book will be available for all eReader devices in addition to home computers, laptops and even some cell phones.

Pricing Your Print Book and eBook

One of the things self publishing authors struggle with the most is the price of their book. They often want to set the price based on the page length or the cost to manufacture the book. Those factors can be taken into consideration, but I recommend pricing the book based on the quality of the story, and what other books in the same category are selling for. Go to bookstores or research online and review books that are similar to yours. What price are they being sold for?

Pricing your eBook works in the same way. Compare it to eBooks that are similar to yours. You might want to do a special sale on your eBook to draw attention to your title and other titles you may have written. Remember that the selling price of the eBook often needs to fall within a certain range to make your eBook eligible for higher royalty amounts. This will vary by retailer.

While the cost should affect some of the decisions you make in the publishing process, remember that ultimately your story is what is most important. It's the quality of your content that will help sell the book, and will help determine the book's worth/selling price.

Bookselling

A variety of options are available for authors to sell their self published works. From Amazon to an author's website, community events to independent bookstores, the avenues for print book and eBook selling are growing daily.

Did you know that 52% of all books are not sold in bookstores? They are sold online, by mail order, in discount or warehouse stores, through book clubs, in non-traditional retail outlets, and more! By brainstorming, an author who is self publishing can come up with lots of ways to sell their books. Online options for print books include Amazon, an author's own website, their publishing support provider's online store (if available), and other online retailers. In their community, an author can work with independent bookstores, other local retailers, museums, sports arenas, community events such as festivals, and any place that could be connected to the subject matter of their book. For eBooks, authors can use Amazon's KDP, Barnes & Noble's PubIt, Smashwords, Google Books, and many others.

Self publishers should explore as many avenues as possible for listing their title. And when doing so, should make sure that they are going to get a fair return for each copy sold, and that they have the option to remove their book from being sold with the seller at any time.

Marketing and Promotion

In this digital era, the methods of promotion available to authors seems endless. Authors should be aware of their target audience and their book's topic when selecting which promotional methods to use.

AUTHOR'S WEBSITE

There are certain basics that should be included in any author's website: a synopsis or piece of the book for viewers to read, author bio, contact information, press kit and shopping cart. But in addition to the basics, consider adding these elements to your site as well: a blog, video of an author interview or reading/signing, discussion questions, bonus content like meet the characters, etc.

SOCIAL MEDIA

Social media tools can be used to promote interaction and discussion with readers and potential readers. Social media options include: Facebook, Twitter, LinkedIn, YouTube and many others. At the minimum, authors should have a Facebook page to share updates, a LinkedIn profile, and a Twitter account.

VIDEO/AUDIO

Video and audio tools are becoming increasingly popular tools for promotion by self publishing authors. Have an author Q&A taped, and have a video book trailer made, and post them on YouTube, Facebook, Twitter, and your website. If you do a reading or book signing, put video and photos of the event on all your social media pages. But remember to keep all video and audio clips and trailers short and sweet. In the digital era, attention spans are shorter!

CAN YOU COMMIT AND MAINTAIN?

The key to promoting your book is to maintain a presence once you've created an identity. If you're not up to speed on the variety of online and social media tools, remember that there will be a learning curve, and that it's perfectly normal. Once you've started using the variety of tools, it's key to make regular updates – that could mean weekly, daily, or even every few hours! When you're interacting directly with your audience, remember that you'll have to take the good with the bad, so be prepared for both compliments and criticism.

So What Does It All Cost?

The cost of self publishing a book is wide-ranging. There are a number of elements that will factor into the total cost. Some are upfront costs to initially publish the book and get the marketing campaign off the ground, and then there may be long-term costs that are more "maintenance" based, such as storage of the book with a distributor, web designer fees, marketing provider's fees, shipping, etc.

Some providers offer packages, others offer their services a la carte, and will work with you to essentially create a custom package that meets your book's needs.

Costs can range anywhere from as low as $299 to as much as $30,000. Essentially, you can't get the minimum needed for the book, including a custom-designed cover and professional layout formatted to fit the feel of your book, for less than $1,500.

Sometimes authors looking to self publish start the process by focusing on how much it will cost to print their book. I like to remind them that having their story edited, determining their target audience, and creating marketing plans should take up the majority of their focus in the publishing process.

Is Your Book a Success?

There are a number of ways to gauge the success of a book. By industry standards, a fiction book is considered successful if it sells 5,000 copies; a nonfiction book is labeled a success when 7,500 copies are sold.

By your standards, are you achieving the goal you set when you decided to publish a book? Has it helped strengthen your brand? Increased awareness of your company's offerings? Brought focus to a social issue? Helped educate youth? Set you apart as an "expert" in your industry? All of these can be measures of successfully publishing a book.

So get writing, and after that, the rest is up to you!

REFERENCES

- *"E-book Sales Explode in February as Other Segments Sink."* <u>Publishers Weekly</u>. *April 14, 2011. http://www.publishersweekly.com/pw/by-topic/digital/retailing/article/46870-e-book-sales-explode-in-february-as-other-segments-sink.html?utm_source = Publishers + Weekly's + PW + Daily &utm_campaign = 0cf8530cca-UA-15906914-1&utm_medium = email*

- *Meyer, Michael. "About that Book Advance…"* <u>NY Times</u>. *(April 10, 2009) Accessed September 15, 2011. http://www.nytimes.com/2009/04/12/books/review/Meyer-t.html*

- *Memmott, Carol. "Authors catch fire with self-published e-books."* <u>USA Today</u>. *(February 9, 2011) Accessed September 15, 2011. http://www.usatoday.com/life/books/news/2011-02-09-ebooks09_ST_N.htm*

- *Ross, Marilyn and Tom. SPR - Self Publishing Resources. http://selfpublishingresources.com/resources/books-news-and-publishing-industry-statistics/*

- *"Traditional Book Output Up 5%; Nontraditional Soars."* <u>Publishers Weekly</u>. *May 18, 2011. http://www.publishersweekly.com/pw/by-topic/industry-news/manufacturing/article/47243-traditional-book-output-up-5--nontraditional-soars.html*

- *U.S. Copyright Office http://www.copyright.gov/help/faq/faq-general.html*

Authors who decide to self publish need to undergo a shift in their thinking. They are no longer a <u>writer</u> or an <u>author</u>, they are now a <u>publisher</u>.

~Ahmad Meradji

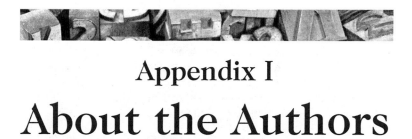

Appendix I
About the Authors

Joan Boneberg
Speech Improvement Resources, LLC

Joan M. Boneberg, M.S., CCC-SLP is a Business Communication Coach, Board Certified Speech Pathologist, speaker, author and President of Speech Improvement Resources, LLC, a business communication firm located in Alpharetta, Georgia. She is a graduate of the State University of New York College at Buffalo where she received her undergraduate and Masters degrees in Speech Pathology.

Her expertise in business communications allows her to customize individual and corporate programs in the areas of "immersion" listening, body language, presentation content and delivery, interviewing, telephone and business writing skills. Joan's coaching experience and client commitment translates these skills into improved client/colleague relationships, sales & productivity and business growth.

Joan has shared her communications expertise in her book, *"Communication Chemistry: 25 Essential Elements to Make You a Compelling Communicator."*

Additionally, Joan is active as a Board Member of the charity Just One Angel, a Vendor Member of the National Speakers Association, member of the Johns Creek Chamber of Commerce as well as other business and speaking organizations in metro Atlanta.

Contact Joan: **www.speakingspecialist.com**

82

Bonnie B. Daneker
Write Advisors

As CEO of Write Advisors, Bonnie B. Daneker oversees the strategic direction of the company to enable its clients to express themselves digitally and in print, using the most appropriate resources to reach their non-fiction publishing goals. Formerly, she was President of BD Donaldson Publishing, Inc., an Atlanta-based publishing company that created and distributed oncology-focused healthcare information. Author of *The Compassionate Caregiver Series*®, Bonnie released her seventh book, *CLIMB*, in November 2010, with Sandy Hofmann, President of Women in Technology (WIT). With WIT, she holds the position of Program Director, Thought Leadership.

She has appeared on television's "The Dream Show" and multiple radio programs. Daneker has been featured in and has contributed to various print and online publications, most notably in her role as Expert Contributor in Oncology Caregiving for Caring.com. Her webinar, "How Writing a Book Can Change Your Career and Your Life" was broadcast in April 2011.

Prior to her work in the publishing industry, Bonnie spent over 10 years in technology consulting. Ever the entrepreneur, she created three successful technology-related startups. She has earned a BA in Journalism from The Ohio State University and an MBA in Strategic Planning and Entrepreneurship from The Goizueta School of Business at Emory University. She and her husband live in Atlanta. When not writing or helping others write, she enjoys volunteering, exercising, and traveling.

Contact Bonnie: **www.writeadvisors.com**
bbdaneker@writeadvisors.com

Robin Hensley
Raising The Bar

Robin Hensley, The Business Development Coach for World Class Rainmakers, is founder and president of Raising the Bar. Ms. Hensley specializes in coaching managing partners and other key law and accounting firm profitability leaders. She is author of the book, *Raising the Bar: Legendary Rainmakers Share Their Business Development Secrets* as well as numerous eBooks, articles and publications.

Ms. Hensley held business development and marketing positions with the Atlanta law firms Kilpatrick Townsend & Stockton LLP and Swift, Currie, McGhee & Hiers, LLP and she was also a CPA with Ernst & Young, serving on both the audit and consulting staffs. She currently serves on the board of directors of Superior Uniform Group, listed on NASDAQ, where she has chaired the audit committee for more than 10 years. She served on the board of directors of Northside Hospital in Atlanta, GA for 10 years.

Her honors include The Atlanta Legal Aid Society Advisory Board, Leadership Atlanta alumna, Honorary Lifetime Member of the Board of the American Cancer Society in metro Atlanta and the *Atlanta Business Chronicle's* "Top 20 Self-Made Women of Atlanta". Her work as a business development coach has been featured in numerous publications, including *Managing Partner Magazine, Journal of Accountancy, National Law Review, Corporate Board Magazine,* the *Atlanta Business Chronicle, Atlanta Journal-Constitution* and the *Daily Report.*

Contact Robin: **www.raisingthebar.com**
rhensley@raisingthebar.com

Vanessa Lowry
Connect 4 Leverage

Vanessa Lowry is an author, entrepreneur, radio host, speaker, graphic designer and marketing consultant. She leverages nearly 30 years of design and marketing expertise to support book authors who are self publishing.

She co-authored *30 Days of Gratitude; Improv to Improve Your Business* and this book, *Publishing as a Marketing Strategy.* Vanessa envisioned these concepts, selected collaborators, co-authored, designed and formatted all three books. Information about Vanessa's new radio show and book project can be found at *www.artasworship.net.*

She is the regular guest host of the radio show *Write Here, Write Now* on the Business RadioX station.

Vanessa has been a featured speaker at business, civic and non-profit groups. A partial listing includes the North Fulton Chamber of Commerce, Kennesaw State University, Georgia Writers Association, Atlanta Theosophical Society, Georgia Center for Non-Profits, Rotary, Kiwanis, American Business Women's Association (ABWA), Johnson Ferry Baptist Women's Retreat and Robert H. Schuller Institute for Successful Church Leadership.

Vanessa loves to learn. She learned the principles of improvisation under the direction of Blank Stage Productions in Marietta, GA. She also has a certification as a reflexologist, a certification in massage and holds the rank of 2nd degree black belt in karate.

Contact Vanessa: **www.connect4leverage.com**
www.artasworship.net
www.linkedin.com/in/VanessaLowry

Ahmad Meradji
BookLogix Publishing Services

Ahmad Meradji has over 25 years of experience in publishing and on-demand printing. He was one of the individuals involved in setting up the first digital book publishing and on-demand printing models at Xerox, later serving as a consultant in the publishing industry.

After moving to Boston from Iran, with dreams of becoming a dentist or an architect, Ahmad completed his B.S. in Architectural Engineering at Wentworth Institute of Technology. He later found himself working in the print industry, taking a position with Xerox in the '80s. He obtained his Masters from Lesley University in 1995 and was a senior manager with Xerox by the time he moved to Atlanta in 2003 to accept a position as a Sr. Vice President with RSM McGladrey an H&R Block Company.

It's always been a dream of Ahmad's to own and operate his own business. In 2006 he co-founded Apex Book Manufacturing. With his extensive knowledge of the printing industry, Ahmad and his business partner, Akash Mangru, established a high-quality print on-demand shop in Alpharetta, GA. Three years later, they saw a growing need for a resource for authors who wanted to self publish their books, and BookLogix Publishing Services was created.

As President and CEO of Booklogix Publishing Services, Ahmad is passionate about helping authors self publish their work, and sharing his extensive knowledge of self publishing and on-demand printing. Ahmad is a frequent public speaker on the topic of self publishing, sharing his insights at a number of universities, conferences, and community events.

Contact Ahmad: **www.booklogix.com**

Anita R. Paul
The Write Image

Anita Paul coaches and mentors corporate professionals and successful entrepreneurs to become published authors. Through her Write Your Life program, she shares strategies for writing, publishing, and marketing a book ... and then leveraging it to upsell your expertise.

A 20-year veteran of the marketing communications industry, Anita started The Write Image in 1997. The Write Image develops marketing and public relations programs for mid-size businesses and organizations. Anita uses her immense planning, organizing, and strategic marketing skills to help clients develop effective communications strategies and public relations campaigns throughout the U.S.

After years of working with decision makers in various industries she realized one thing they had in common – they were "secret agents." These super intelligent, well respected, knowledgeable leaders were experts in their fields, but nobody knew it. She wondered, what would help these experts get noticed? The answer: Every expert needs a book of her own. So she developed a program to help professionals upsell their expertise. Over the years, her passion for mentoring authors to overcome obstacles to their publishing success became her focus, and thus, Write Your Life was created.

Anita is the author of three books: *Take the Mystery Out of Marketing* (2002), *What Goes Around Comes Around* (a novel), and *Write Your Life: Create Your Ideal Life And the Book You've Been Wanting to Write* (2011). As a freelance writer, her articles have appeared in over 25 trade publications in the U.S. and Canada.

Contact Anita: **www.thewriteimage.net**
www.writeyourlife.net

Appendix II
Other Contributors

The information in this section is from business professionals who answered this question on LinkedIn:

In what ways has publishing a book helped you market your business?

Answers printed with permission.

Diane Marentette
http://www.linkedin.com/pub/diane-marentette/6/44b/90a

Publishing our book has had a number of positive impacts on promoting our business.

1. Writing the book helped us shift our perspective about our business.

2. Many of our clients had asked "where can we read more about this when you are not here" (meaning our unique perspective) so there was already some appetite for it.

3. Having a published book available to support our work has invited more interest in our point of view.

4. This one surprises us - people want an autographed book! Offering that draws people's attention!

5. Our clients like that we are "award winning authors" of a business book!

Although we do not depend upon the book for anything, we have really liked having it written and available. It captures some of our thinking that we use in our business and our lives in ways that obviously pay off!

Melinda Hamilton Schmiedeknecht
http://www.linkedin.com/in/mizschmitty

My colleague, David Alexander, has published a book (co-authored with the founder of BNI, Dr. Ivan Misner, and Atlanta-based marketing guru Brian Hilliard.) Although I'm not the author of *Networking Like A Pro*, I'm reaping the benefits of this book. We have a corporate training program based on it and the fact that it hit #1 on Amazon. com gives credibility to the program.

Rob Duncan
http://ca.linkedin.com/in/robduncan

As a professional speaker, writing books has helped me in several ways, including:

1. It helped me organize and crystallize my thinking on areas of expertise that I had been teaching and speaking about for a while.

2. Nothing helps book a speaking engagement more than being "author of." It puts you into a different league from beginning speakers and people who speak occasionally.

3. The books make a great keepsake for people who attend training and speaking events. It is easy to build a "free book for all participants" into a quote at an attractive price. This can be a distinguishing feature for a competitive proposal.

4. People enjoy having books signed by the author, and this can be a great way to build a deeper bond with audience members and training participants.

5. A book is a terrific shorthand introduction to your capabilities, and can almost be used as a "business card" for prospects. It is also easy to send a copy along to media interviewers, providing a good focal point for a discussion.

Wallace Jackson
http://www.linkedin.com/in/wallacejackson

Establishment of Expertise Internationally.

Lisa Earle McLeod
http://www.linkedin.com/in/lisaearlemcleod

Nothing builds your credibility faster than sending a signed copy of your hard cover book to the CEO or VP. They don't even have to read it, you have already established yourself as an expert.

It also ups your speaking fees, but only if you have a mainstream publisher and you have some mentions in the press.

PS: Plus you can put it on your signature line.

Lara Solomon
http://au.linkedin.com/in/larasolomon

I self published, but I get A LOT of comments on how professional it looks, I think that now it doesn't matter if you self publish or not.

With my book I found that:

- It increased my credibility

- It made me stand out

- I was perceived to be more of an expert

- It promotes my brand

- It makes people look twice at me

There is that saying that everyone has a book in them, but in reality not many actually get around to writing one. I think that people perceive it to be a lot of hard work and so are exceptionally impressed by those who have done it.

Francesca Bonner
http://uk.linkedin.com/in/fbonner

I would say that publishing a book can also be used as a long term marketing strategy. I don't think it has to be based on expertise. It could be a book of great full clients quotes as proof of your skills.

If you have a holiday company, for example, you could leave one in each room/house – a beautiful book with photos and reviews of other holidays you offer. If your clients have been enjoying the holiday they are on, then they may book somewhere else the following year.

You could also create a coffee table book which you give as a gift to your best clients. It would create goodwill with them and be a lovely book that their guests will pick up and look at – subliminal marketing – to keep your name out there and create some noise about it.

Regardless, it is essential that books are produced to a professional standard, self published or not.

Sue Edwards
http://uk.linkedin.com/in/virtualassistant5

I agree with many of these answers and particularly with Lara's comments. I am a virtual assistant and the minute I mention self publishing my book, people take more interest and ask questions. I'm now starting to help others self publish too.

There isn't much profit to be made from a book for the amount of work involved unless you diversify and give presentations etc. However I enjoy the challenge and am now working on the next one.

Patrick McFadden
http://www.linkedin.com/pub/patrick-mcfadden/24/126/22

1. **Communication:** Having a book is a wonderful way to communicate your message to a broader audience. If you are a speaker or teacher you can exponentially increase your audience with a book. If you have any area of expertise, a book can help you leverage that expertise. Writing a book will help you find your own voice. It will help you trust that you have something important to say. You have a message that must be told. A true writer is someone who cannot not write. I didn't start out wanting to be a bestselling author – I started by struggling with people who were trying to find meaning in their work and wanted to share those principles with more people.

2. **Fame:** Yes, there is a certain amount of celebrity status that comes instantly with having a published book. Many sports, political, and media figures have arranged to have a book about them or their field of knowledge. A book says that you have moved up the ladder significantly. A book will leave a legacy of thought and insight that will hopefully continue long after you are gone. It's a thrill to run into someone in an airport, on a cruise ship or at the mall who has read your book. And you'll get emails from people on the other side of the world who have been impacted by reading your words on a page.

3. **Fortune:** Okay, we certainly hear about the John Grishams, Dan Browns, Joel Osteens and Rick Warrens of the world – where sales of their books made them millionaires over and over. But recognize how extremely rare that is. It does happen but the odds are stacked against you. There are lots of ways to make money more easily than hoping it will come from a book – but keep planning for it to happen to you.

4. **Credibility:** A book does help to position you as an expert in your field. If you are a consultant, speaker, coach, pastor or trainer, having a book is a valuable tool for establishing your credibility as a person who is an expert.

I tend to view my book as powerful business cards for drawing people into the other aspects of our McFadden Coaching business.

Mitch Carnell
http://www.linkedin.com/in/mitchcarnell

I published a small book, *Say Something Nice; Be a Lifter.* It fostered my speaking and training career, became the basis for *Say Something Nice Day* on June first each year which is now listed in the Chase Calendar of Events. We now also have *Say Something Nice Sunday* on the first Sunday in June which is now celebrated by churches in the US and UK.

Roberto Blake
http://www.linkedin.com/in/robertoblake

Publishing a book whether traditionally or as an eBook is a great way to build credibility and exposure. The sales don't even have to be impressive, completing and publishing a book puts you in a minority among people and even among professionals.

It demonstrates your knowledge, level of commitment in your field, and your ambition. All very positive and impressive things that set you apart in people's minds when they are qualifying you versus someone else.

Bernadette Boas

http://www.linkedin.com/in/bernadetteboas

The beauty of publishing a book is that it gives you over a year (or two) of marketing opportunities for the book. The moment I conceived the book topic – I started marketing it. First reason was to validate the concept, then to gather the 'value proposition' from my target market, then I used it to confirm my title, my cover, and more. All along I pulled the reader to it. More importantly, I used the marketing of it from day one to commit myself to the project.

As far as impact on my business? From the beginning, long before it was published, I was being asked to speak on the subject, was asked by bloggers to contribute content, deployed articles on portals, and more.

So yes, publishing a book has tremendous value on one's business.

A final note – my book also created my second business – Ball of Fire, Inc. Because of the marketing and publishing of the book (August 1), followers and fans have requested programs, educational products, retreats, merchandise, and even media (TV, radio) opportunities.

The book – *Shedding the Corporate Bitch* is my personal story of how my own angst, attitude, fears, and negative mindset created a persona of a bitch, as a way to climb the corporate ladder and obtain position, power and prosperity. Then it severely impacted my career, relationships, health and life. My transformation and journey is now helping men and women to discover, confront and shed their own bitches (angst, attitude, fears, and negative mindset), so they can create the riches life has to offer them.

Every one of us have a story within us that would benefit someone else – therefore writing a book is good for the heart, soul, mind and business!!!!

Myra McElhaney
http://www.linkedin.com/in/myramcelhaney

With the first anthology book that I participated in years ago I was surprised at how being an 'author' increased the perception of my credibility. Clients seemed more willing to schedule me to speak and train. Having subsequent books gives fresh reasons for publicity and to contact clients for additional bookings.

Appendix III
Tips

10 Tips on Working with Collaborators

by Bonnie B. Daneker

Adding ideas or expertise from others can greatly enhance your book project. However, being involved in a collaboration can sometimes be tricky. Follow these tips to make your process smoother and your results more in line with your objectives:

1. Be clear on what you're trying to achieve, so everyone is on the same page with goals.

2. Decide early who will be the "lead" on the project. There can be only one; this is the person who "breaks ties" or ends arguments.

3. Have a conversation about what strengths and interest each party has. Try to match those with the work that needs to be done.

4. Be flexible. Sometimes you may not get to work on what you like but what the book needs.

5. Create timelines with extra time built in. Life happens, and you may be glad you added cushion.

6. When you have criticism, try to deliver it in a productive way. A good rule of thumb is not to say "I don't like it" without having a reason why and an alternate solution. This goes for everything, from approach to edits to distribution.

7. Communicate. We all know what happens when you assume.

8. Pitch in. You may be asked to do something extra or different in the course of the project. Keep the end in mind.

9. Remember, a collaboration is like a marriage. There may be ups and downs, but focus on the end goals and you can achieve them. However, if your differences are insurmountable, you may need to part ways.

10. After the book is finished, recognize your collaborators every way you can. Success breeds success, and you may be asked by others to contribute to projects for bigger and more valuable exposure.

As CEO of Write Advisors, **Bonnie B. Daneker** *oversees the strategic direction of the company to enable its clients to express themselves digitally and in print, using the most appropriate resources to reach their non-fiction publishing goals.* **www.WriteAdvisors.com**

6-Step Recipe for Writing Your Book

by Anita R. Paul

One of the most difficult things about writing a book is organizing your thoughts. If you're like most writers you have notebooks full of ideas and shoeboxes full of notes with scribbled outlines, dialogue, tips, and descriptions. You've got the content right there in those shoeboxes ... so what do you do with it?

Approach writing your book like you would approach preparing an extravagant meal for some very special guests – your readers. There's a process, right? Let's use our meal preparation analogy to walk through the basic steps of writing your book.

STEP 1: KNOW YOUR GUESTS

You want to "wow" them with this meal and cause them to ask for seconds. So, based on what you know about them, what are their preferences? Do they like spicy foods, lots of sauces, cheesy dishes, salt-free fare, a little chocolate, steamed, fried, grilled, or broiled?

In the same way, consider your ideal readers. What are they looking for in a book like yours? Interesting anecdotes, useful tips, moving dialogue, emotional scenes, honest expression, life lessons, a love scene, a villain with a conscience, a moral to the story? You probably have all of these in that shoebox in your closet. So dig it out and start searching through those notes.

STEP 2: CREATE YOUR RECIPE

Typically, you would find a recipe in a cookbook or perhaps from a trusted cook ... or sometimes you have to make it up yourself. For your book, this recipe is called an outline. You need to determine the main theme of your book, the characters, the setting, the moral or lessons of the story, the key points and tips. Then decide what comes first, next, and last in your book.

Every line, every character, every bit of dialogue, every scene, every concept should focus on the theme. You decide how much of anything to include (such as tips, drama, dialogue, backstory, characters), how long a scene should simmer, at what temperature you should allow a memory to bake, and how long the lessons of life should cool on the rack.

STEP 3: SELECT THE INGREDIENTS

Next, let's gather the ingredients. Oh wait, you've got them right there is those shoeboxes full of notes and ramblings that you've been collecting. Shop for the meat, the potatoes, the spices, seasonings, garnish, and even the perfect wine to accompany your meal. Find them in your notes. Read through what you've already written and determine how all of that fits into your recipe. Also, you'll want to take the time to browse through the supermarket ... in this instance, the library, your own bookshelf or an online bookseller. Remember, writers read. Reading is the process of shopping, as it were, for style, context, ideas, voice, and technique. Develop your own unique work of art, so you don't need to snag another author's words, characters, or theme verbatim.

Make sure you use quality ingredients: interesting characters, moving dialogue, action, descriptive words, engaging scenes, valuable tips, step-by-step instruction, a moral or lesson that readers can easily grasp, and of course a theme that is carried through the entire book. No scene, resource, conversation, or character should be included that doesn't directly influence the overall theme of your book.

STEP 4: PREPARE CAREFULLY

There is an art to preparing a delicious meal. You assemble your ingredients, read through that recipe once again, ensure you have all of the equipment and utensils needed, and you go at it. You chop, you measure, you taste. It's a process, remember. With your writing, you add a dab of dialogue, a pinch of persuasion, and a little laughter. Be the sous-chef and make certain that you have everything you need to craft this delicious meal.

STEP 5: LEARN THE ART OF PRESENTATION

Your guests smelled the savory aromas when they walked through the door. For your book, the cover art or the title gets readers to grab your book off the shelf. But what's inside is what gets them to want more. It's all about presentation.

Have you ever been presented with a meal or a dish that looked ... well ... unappealing? It may smell yummy and be delicious to the taste, but if the presentation is all wrong you might think twice about tasting it. Consider that with your book layout and design, as well as with your promotional information.

Technical aspects of writing – grammar, punctuation, spelling, voice, tense – as well as layout, format, publishing options, or cover design all play a huge part in the appearance of your book. Whether you self publish or outsource, don't leave your book in the hands of others. Oversee the entire process yourself.

STEP 6: SHARE AND ENJOY

Delicious food is scrumptious even if you eat it alone. However, when shared with family, friends, and other guests, the meal can be that much more delectable. Marketing and promoting your book and you, as an author, is vital to making sure that as many people as possible can enjoy the yummy vittles you've prepared and are ready to serve up. You have a story to tell. There are hundreds of thousands — dare I say, millions — of people who want and need to know your story, the lessons you've learned, the tips you have, and the knowledge you've gained. Don't leave them waiting. Your guests have arrived ... and their appetites are voracious. Bon appetit!

Anita R. Paul, Author's Coach, Writer Extradonaire, and President of The Write Image, mentors corporate professionals and successful entrepreneurs to upsell their expertise by becoming a published author, and then to leverage their book for their success. She can be reached at www.writeyourlife.net and at www.thewriteimage.net.

10 Tips for Working with a Graphic Designer

by Vanessa Lowry

If you are self publishing, you have creative control over the look of your final book, as well as responsibility for marketing and promotion after publication.

How do you decide which graphic professional will be a good fit to design your cover and format your book's interior? Your printer/publisher may have an in-house designer or you may know other authors who will share a referral. It is important that you have clear communication from the beginning with the graphic designer you choose. Ask lots of questions and listen to the questions the designer asks you. Get feedback from authors who have worked with this particular designer.

Keep in mind that a designer with more expertise may offer greater value. Even if they charge a higher hourly rate, they may work more quickly, have better ideas and be a more effective collaborator with you.

A wider variety of proof options requires more design hours and equates to a higher investment to get the files of your book ready to print. Major changes to the content of your manuscript after design has begun can escalate the time required to complete your project and your final invoice will reflect that.

Come prepared with answers to these questions when meeting with your graphic designer:

1. Who is the target buyer for your book? Having a specific target reader will guide you while writing your book and will make it easier when marketing. For example: *All business professionals* is too broad a description of your target reader. Your narrow niche might be *CFOs of companies with over $10 million in revenues.*

2. What other book covers appeal to you that sell to a similar target reader? Have a few examples to show.

3. If you want the cover to include an illustration, photograph or graphic, what kind of image do you have in mind? Do you already own a high-resolution file of the image you want to use or will your designer need to research images? What amount have you budgeted for licensing the image you approve?

4. What is the feeling you want your book cover to create for the reader?

5. Are there particular colors you prefer for the cover? Do you want it to tie into the colors of your company's branding?

6. What size do you want your finished book to be? Do other books in your niche typically publish as a soft cover book or as a hardcover book?

7. Have you chosen a printer/publisher? What is the contact information for the person with whom your designer will coordinate for design specifications and deadlines?

8. What is your anticipated completion date? Do you have a trade show, event or marketing opportunity on the horizon for which you would like to have printed books?

As a guideline: After editing of your manuscript is complete, allow 10 - 12 weeks for cover design, formatting of your book and galley proofs through delivery of your first shipment of printed books. Your designer may be able to shorten this time frame if you communicate your needs clearly at the beginning.

9. Who else will be included in your decision process? Some authors want to build excitement for their book by soliciting feedback on book titles or cover design from a select group of their followers. Others want a faster turnaround and limit their feedback to only two or three trusted advisors.

10. What is my budget? Have I done enough research to know what others have invested in design, formatting and printing in self publishing a similar book? Your designer should be able to give you a fee range based on their experience of working on other books similar in size and scope to yours.

Vanessa Lowry is an author, radio host, speaker, graphic designer and marketing consultant. She leverages nearly 30 years of design and marketing expertise to support book authors who are self publishing. **www.connect4leverage.com**

12 Ways to Keep Your Nonfiction Book in the News

by Sandra Beckwith

Publishers are willing to publicize nonfiction books when they're released, but they rarely do much after the launch to keep books in the news, even though most deserve ongoing media exposure. Here are some easy things you can do to generate continuing publicity for your title. Use a mix of these ideas to develop a 12-month publicity plan that will provide the support your book needs.

1. **Turn the advice in your chapters into a series of monthly tip sheets.** A tip sheet is a press release that offers tips or advice in a bulleted or numbered format. Start your tip sheet with an introductory paragraph that explains why the tips you're offering are important, list your bulleted advice, then tie it all together at the end with a concluding paragraph. Send it to appropriate media outlets; the distribution list will depend on your topic.

2. **Contact the press immediately when your topic is making headlines to offer your expert perspective.** This is a sure thing with most local media outlets when it's a national news story because you're giving them a local angle. Fax or e-mail (no attachments) your bio and a cover letter explaining your position on the breaking news to the appropriate media contact. If you've done

enough interviews to prepare for the big time, pitch the national news outlets, too.

3. **Add the media to your newsletter distribution list.** The same useful advice or information you offer subscribers in your print or electronic newsletter could be of interest to reporters covering that topic, too. I got a book contract several years ago from the publicity that resulted from adding the media to the distribution list of a newsletter I publish.

4. **Repackage your book content into by-lined trade magazine articles.** Depending on the terms of your publishing contract, you might need to do some rewriting so it's "new" material. Make sure the author credit at the end of the article includes your book title.

5. **Capitalize on holidays and special months, weeks and days by distributing a press release with useful, newsworthy information related to the topic, or by contacting the press to offer yourself as an expert information source.** For example, many daily newspapers run articles in December about how the holidays are especially difficult for people who are grieving the recent loss of a loved one or facing the anniversary of a loss. This presents many coast-to-coast interview opportunities for the author of a book on grief and loss – but only if the author reaches out to the press.

6. **Contact the public relations department of your industry's trade association to offer yourself for media interviews.** Association public relations people are often contacted by writers like us looking for members with a particular expertise to interview. Make sure your association knows about your qualifications and the topics you can comment on, and you'll get referral calls.

7. **Conduct a newsworthy and relevant survey on your topic and announce the interesting results in a press release.** The author of a cookbook designed to make cooking simple and easy can survey people about why they don't cook more, and release the findings in a press release sent to newspaper food editors and cooking magazines. The release should include information about your book's connection to the survey topic.

8. **Sponsor an attention-getting contest and announce the results in a press release.** To promote my humor book about men, I conducted a "Worst Gift from a Man Contest." The resulting press release led to nationwide media attention, including a holiday appearance on a national cable TV talk show.

9. **Push your publisher's publicist to monitor ProfNet for reporter queries related to your topic all year.** Alternatively, subscribe to ProfNet via its PR Leads reseller and respond to appropriate queries. A $99 per month subscription via www.prleads.com is more affordable than a ProfNet subscription.

10. **Monitor writer forums for source requests.** Members frequently post requests on the magazines and newspapers forum for interview sources.

11. **Tell the media when you're visiting their market.** Reporters love to interview experts who aren't local, so if you're in another city for any reason, contact the appropriate media people two weeks before your trip to offer ideas for articles they can write based on an in-person interview with you. If you're in town to speak, send an announcement press release several weeks in advance and offer to do a pre-event telephone interview.

12. **Repurpose your best tips into a free booklet.** Write and distribute a press release that describes the booklet and how people can get a free copy; make sure both the booklet and the release include information about your book, too.

Generating ongoing publicity is work, but it's not rocket science. Invest the time so you boost sales while contributing to your author platform. You'll see the rewards at the end of the year.

Sandra Beckwith offers a free book publicity and promotion e-zine at www.buildbookbuzz.com and teaches the "Book Publicity 101: How to Build Book Buzz" e-course.

30 Ways to Market Your Book Before and After Publication

by Vanessa Lowry

Have FUN and find ways to have conversations on-line and in person.

1. **Add your author credential to your email signature.** Before you publish, your signature can be "Author of the forthcoming book, [the working title of your book].

2. **Write a short synopsis of your book, an author bio and get a professional headshot.**

3. **Engage your Tribe.** Ask an exclusive group of supporters to vote on your book title or cover designs.

4. **Create a book trailer and post it on YouTube.** See sample book trailers here:
   http://www.squidoo.com/booktrailers
   http://www.youtube.com/watch?v=rMhgO2m8DxM

5. **Create a Facebook book fan page.**

6. **Have a website (or blog site) for you and/or your book.** Set up a free site at Wordpress.com.

7. **Develop a list of discussion questions that book clubs or other groups can use as a basis of talking about your book.** Create a page on your website for this information.

8. **Set up a Google Alert for your name, your book name and your book topic.** Find out how here: *www.buildbookbuzz.com/tips/*

9. **Have a business card, bookmark or postcard printed for your book to use as a handout.** Add a Quick Response (QR) code that points back to your launch page with a special offer, Facebook fan page or book trailer.

10. **Develop an email list of potential readers and start sending updates before and after you publish through an email newsletter.** Companies like *ConstantContact.com* and *MailChimp.com* make it easy.

11. **Build relationships with bloggers related to your topics.** Join discussions in which your target reader participates. Use Google Blogsearch *(www.google.com/blogsearch)*, *Alltop.com* and *Technorati.com* to find the people who'd likely blog related to your subject matter.

12. **Create a pre-publication offer.**

13. **Post a question on LinkedIn related to your book topic and respond with at least a thank you email to all who post an answer.** Use some of the answers in blog posts and in your email newsletters after getting permission from the respondents.

14. **Set up an account in the Author Program of Goodreads.com and create a giveaway for your book.** You can specify how many copies of your book will be given away.

15. **Find opportunities to cross promote other authors.** If you are both publishing at the same time to a similar target reader, add a sample chapter at the end of one another's books.

16. **Create fun videos!** Shoot a video as you open the box with your first printed books, a video of your first sighting of your book in a bookstore, a thank you video for all the people who helped launch your book.

17. **Set up a Virtual Book Tour.** Give away copies of your book to targeted bloggers and contacts at media outlets to generate interviews and book reviews. Read more about how to create a virtual book tour in this pdf download: *http://buildbookbuzz.com/virtual-book-tour-basics/*

18. **Sign up free and receive daily emails with queries from reporters, radio hosts and authors searching for sources.** *www.HelpAReporter.com* (HARO) and *www.ReporterConnection.com*

19. **Use Twitter Search to find people who talk about the topics covered in your book.** Hashtag your posts so others can find you. You can also set up a Twitter Alert. (See link on number 8 of this list.)

20. **Write a guest blog post that provides information or inspiration to readers interested in your book topic or genre.** Approach a blogger who addresses your target reader and offer it as a guest post. If you have a blog, trade guest posts with another blogger in your target market.

21. **Partner with entrepreneurs for companion products.**

22. **Create a 20-minute business presentation that ties into your book topic and promote it to business groups such as Rotary and Kiwanis groups.** Don't talk about your book — choose a topic that solves a problem and is related to your book.

23. **Partner with a non-profit to host a book signing or help promote your book launch in exchange for a percentage of sale proceeds within a designated period of time.**

24. **Find individuals, companies or organizations who would want to purchase your book in quantity.** Have multi-packs that can be ordered on-line and/or create a pdf with details to send to companies.

25. **Contact your hometown library and offer to do a book signing.**

26. **Send press releases to key media contacts at publications that fit your target reader and to your hometown newspaper.** Here are tips on how to do that effectively: *http://www.chriskridler.com/?p=146*

27. **Post press releases on-line** at paid sites like *PRWeb.com* or find a list of free PR posting sites here: *http://www.bookmarket.com/onlinepr.htm.*

28. **Check internet radio sites (like *BlogTalkRadio.com, EmpowerRadio.com* or *BusinessRadioX.com*) for shows that relate to your topic.** Send the host a concise email with why you would be an ideal guest.

29. **Host a meet up and post photos on your social media sites.**

30. **Give your "tribe" links to share on your book journey.** Share pre-order specials, launch info, interview links, press release links, videos and more. Encourage people within your tribe to have conversations with you. Respond to comments and emails.

Vanessa Lowry is an author, radio host, speaker, graphic designer and marketing consultant. She leverages nearly 30 years of design and marketing expertise to support book authors who are self publishing. www.connect4leverage.com

Appendix IV
Blogs, Websites, & Podcasts

Websites and Blogs

Write Lean
http://writeyourlifeblog.blogspot.com/2011/09/write-lean.html

----

Getting Mileage Out of Your Book: Repurpose the Content
http://writeyourlifeblog.blogspot.com/2011/09/getting-mileage-out-of-your-book.html

----

Tools for the Writer
http://annewainscott.com/tools-writer

Editing, Grammar, Reference
http://www.kennesaw.edu/careersinwriting/resources.html

Build Book Buzz Tip Sheets and Resources
http://buildbookbuzz.com/tips/
http://buildbookbuzz.com/resources/

The Publicity Hound
http://publicityhound.com/publicity-products/free.html

Publishing Workshops, Events and Contests
www.booklogix.com

Writer's Digest Webinars
http://www.writersdigestshop.com/category/ondemand-webin
ars?r=wdnavwebinardownloads

Tribal Author
http://tribalauthor.com/

An Author's Plan for Social Media Efforts by Chris Brogan
http://www.chrisbrogan.com/author-social-media/

Guy Kawasaki's blog posts about launching a book or product
http://mashable.com/2011/03/30/product-launch-social-media/

http://www.openforum.com/articles/how-to-use-facebook-to-
enchant-your-customers

----

9 Ways to Launch a Book by Michael Stelzner
http://www.socialmediaexaminer.com/9-ways-to-use-social-
media-to-launch-a-book/#more-10455

10 Reasons to Write Your Business Book Now
http://www.writingwhitepapers.com/blog/2008/11/03/10-
book-benefits/

Seth Godin's Advice for Authors
http://sethgodin.typepad.com/seths_blog/2006/08/advice_
for_auth.html

Podcasts

Robin Hensley is exclusive Executive Coach for *Business to Business* Magazine. Listen to podcasts and download transcripts on a variety of business development topics on Robin's website.

These topics may be of particular interest as you decide whether publishing a book is the best move for you and your business.

- How to Leverage Your Unique Advantage: An Interview with author and brand marketing expert Robin Fisher Roffer
- Setting goals
- Staying on target/achieving your goals

http://www.raisingthebar.com/info/podcasts.html

Vanessa Lowry is the regular guest host of the internet radio show *Write Here, Write Now.* Tim Morrison and co-host Stone Payton, with Vanessa guest hosting once a month, interview local business people about the book they have written or the book which they intend to write someday. All shows are archived and can be downloaded free.

http://writeherewritenow.businessradiox.com/shows/

Leveraging a Book into Speaking Opportunities

Guests discuss how they have leveraged their published book into speaking opportunities and expanded business offerings. Authors Sandy Weaver Carman, Bernadette Boas and Charlie Cummins are guests.

SHOW AIRED NOVEMBER 22, 2011
http://writeherewritenow.businessradiox.com/shows/

From Blog to Book

Vince Rogers uses blogging to promote his business and has created a book out of the best of his blogs: *The Very Best of Disguised Limits*. Vince shares the impact writing a book has had on his business.

SHOW AIRED SEPTEMBER 13, 2011
http://writeherewritenow.businessradiox.com/shows/

Effectively Using the "Power of the Pen"

Today's guests have mastered the power of the pen and discuss how they use it in their careers. Chuck Reaves, founder of SalesSSuites, has written seven books and numerous white papers. Tim Fulton publishes his own award-winning electronic monthly newsletter, *Small Business Matters*, for small business owners.

SHOW AIRED AUGUST 23, 2011
http://writeherewritenow.businessradiox.com/shows/

Six Degrees of Separation in Writing and Publishing.

Guests discuss how they have tapped into the power of their network of friends, family, colleagues and contacts to connect with key people. They share stories of creating content, publishing their books and getting the word out, all with a little help from their friends.

Listen in as Joan Boneberg, Myra McElhaney and Walter Lawrence share their stories and insights.

SHOW AIRED AUGUST 9, 2011
http://writeherewritenow.businessradiox.com/shows/

Business Leaders Who Write More Than One Book

Gregory Evans, once known as the World's Number one computer hacker, founded National Cyber Security. He has written 8 books; each one discusses different aspects of high-tech security issues. He shares his story on writing more than one book and the impact that has had on his businesses.

SHOW AIRED AUGUST 2, 2011
http://writeherewritenow.businessradiox.com/shows/

Publishing in Collaboration

Writing and publishing a book can be a lonely effort, but it doesn't have to be. Rob Duncan, Barbara Giamanco and Bonnie Daneker discuss their experience of publishing in collaboration with one or more co-authors. Find out some of the benefits of publishing with others and what challenges you may need to overcome.

SHOW AIRED JULY 19, 2011
http://writeherewritenow.businessradiox.com/shows/

Repurposing Your Career

Guests share how they used their careers to become authors. Peter Bowerman transformed a successful copywriting career into becoming an author. He has now written three books: *The Well-Fed Writer; The Well-Fed Writer: Back for Seconds*; and *The Well-Fed Self-*

Publisher: How to Turn One Book into a Full-Time Living. Mike Pniewski has appeared in hundreds of films, TV shows, commercial and industrial films, then wrote *When Life Gives You Lemons, Throw'em Back!: How to Create the Life You Want, No Matter What Comes Your Way.*

SHOW AIRED MAY 24, 2011
http://writeherewritenow.businessradiox.com/shows/

Expanding Your Niche

Publishing a book can attract ideal clients. Find out how organizing expert and consultant Jessica D. Chapman has used her book, *The Entrepreneurial Itch: A Practical Guide to Launching or Refining Your Business* to expand her business niche.

SHOW AIRED MAY 10, 2011
http://writeherewritenow.businessradiox.com/shows/

Publishing and Sales

Renee Walkup has authored two books: *Selling to Anyone Over the Phone* and *The Naked Sales Person.* She shares with listeners what motivated her to write her first book and then why a second book became a must. BookLogix in conjunction with Apex Book Manufacturing helps writers publish their books. Ahmad Meradji tells of how his dream of a company to help writers publish became a reality.

SHOW AIRED MAY 3, 2011
http://writeherewritenow.businessradiox.com/shows/

Review the full archive to listen to past episodes of *Write Here, Write Now* radio. Listen live every Tuesday at 10am Eastern at **http://writeherewritenow.businessradiox.com.**

Thanks for your interest.

Contact any of the authors if you have additional questions.

Joan Boneberg
www.speakingspecialist.com

Bonnie Daneker
www.writeadvisors.com

Robin Hensley
www.raisingthebar.com

Vanessa Lowry
www.connect4leverage.com

Ahmad Meradji
www.booklogix.com

Anita Paul
www.thewriteimage.net